WineMine
A First Anthology

Anthony Hogg shares a joke with André Simon after the fiftieth meeting of Peter Dominic's Wine Mine Club

GUY GRAVETT

WineMine
A First Anthology

EDITED BY ANTHONY HOGG

SOUVENIR PRESS

First British edition published 1970 by Souvenir Press Ltd.,
95, Mortimer Street, London, W.1. and simultaneously in
Canada by The Ryerson Press, Toronto 2, Canada

ISBN 0·285·50297·2

Cover photographs by Guy Gravett.

A night scene in Beaune. Chevaliers du Tastevin at a Château Clos
Vougeot banquet.
A stone Bacchus in a Saumur courtyard.
The window display of Bordeaux's Restaurant Dubern; the
Maison du Vin and other buildings on the opposite side of
Alleés Tourny are reflections.
The cellar of the Hospice de Beaune; the wines in these casks
were those auctioneered the following day in November 1969.
An old vintage plaque, reset in a modern wall, near St. Emilion.

ANDRE SIMON R.I.P.

This book had virtually gone to Press when, on Saturday
September 5 1970, Andrè Simon died. The frontispiece
photograph, taken outside Peter Dominic's Orange Street,
Haymarket branch as we bade him farewell after celebrating the
Fiftieth meeting of The Wine Mine Club in the spring, may well
be the last taken of him at a wine function.

Likewise, writing the foreword to this book was among the last of
many acts of kindness he rendered to friends and acquaintances,
during his long life. How sad that we cannot now all meet him on
his 100th birthday to drink those 1945 clarets, which he declared
he would keep for that occasion!

Designed by David Paul Design Group, Chichester
Filmset by Vantage, Southampton
Printed by W. & J. Jarvis, East Grinstead

Foreword by André Simon

In September 1939, when war was declared, all wine-merchants in the British Isles knew that there was no likelihood of wine being imported until some time after the war, and that they must go out of business or nurse their existing stocks so that they might last as long as the war. Paul Dauthieu was at the time salesman of a firm of London wine-merchants. Sales and salesman had to be checked. Paul was given the sack and £100. Sheer folly, as I thought at the time, he started a modest wine shop in Horsham. He knew—and I did not know then—that nothing is impossible to him who has the will to win, the brain, and the luck: he had them all . . . Many old firms of wine merchants disappeared during the war, but there was one, born in 1939, which flourished: and is still flourishing as Peter Dominic, the name that Paul Dauthieu gave it as being easier to pronounce and remember than his own.

One day, some time after the war, as I was congratulating Paul on his well deserved but near miraculous success, I added: 'You have more than your fair share of gifts, but, of course, you cannot have them all. You can tell a tale better than anybody I know, but you cannot write plain, lucid, attractive and convincing English. If you can get the right man who has the gift of expression in prose, he can, and he will bring to you hundreds—may be thousands of new customers. Paul agreed and asked me to look out for the right man, since I was so much more in touch with writers than he was. Soon afterwards in 1956, Lieutenant Commander Anthony Hogg R.N. wrote to me, knowing that I had many friends and contacts in the Wine Trade, saying he was about to retire and learn the wine trade as a 10s a week apprentice. I did not know him at all well, but I knew that he could write because I had read and published articles of his in the Wine and Food Society's Magazine WINE AND FOOD. Surely, I thought, here is the man for Paul Dauthieu.

And write he did! From 1957 to 1961, there were those almost weekly advertisements, Peter Dominic's Wineyard, front page of the Times, and so on, as well, of course, as a voluminous correspondence to strangers who became customers. Business grew apace and Hogg was made Sales Director. In 1960, the Financial Times described Peter Dominic as 'the private Company which has perhaps done more than any other to fit wine to the English palate and pocket since the war.'

In 1963, a take-over was arranged with the International Distillers and Vintners but Peter Dominic continued independently until 1968, when IDV's 350 shops were merged under one name: Peter Dominic.

However, what is, in my opinion, Anthony Hogg's most original, most remarkable, as well as valuable achievement is WINEMINE. Most wine merchants print a Wine List, giving the names and prices of the wines and spirits they offer for sale, but I am quite sure that it never occurred to any of them that the sale of their wine list to the public on Smith's bookstalls could ever be anything than sheer fiction and nonsense. Incredible as it may appear, it is now a fact. In 1959, a somewhat super Wine List was published by Peter Dominic, giving interesting information about people and places where some of the wines had come from. It was called WINEMINE because it was meant to be a mine of 'Wine, Wit and Wisdom for the Million'. This is what WINEMINE soon became when friendly and knowledgeable writers offered articles dealing with wine from many different angles so that now WINEMINE is a greatly appreciated and widely read journal, the first half of it wine articles and the second half Peter Dominic's Wine List with commentaries. I am told, and I have every reason to believe, that there are now over 150,000 copies of each number printed, many of them sold at the advertised price of 2s, to the public, and many given to the firm's regular customers. What an achievement! WINEMINE must have made a greater number of people in the British Isles take a greater interest in wine, and nothing could have been of greater service to the whole of the Wine Trade!

Mes très sincères félicitations!

André L. Simon

Introduction by Anthony Hogg

Should anybody, never having heard of WINEMINE, chance to buy this book, I must explain that WINEMINE is half a magazine and half a price list. Like Kipling's epithets for the Royal Marines, it could be called 'A kind of giddy harum frodite' or 'A blooming cosmopolouse' of 'All the World's Wines', whose primary aim has always been to inform—with as much 'Wine, Wit and Wisdom' as its amateur editor can pack into some 150 pages.

Inevitably the ten year tale of WINEMINE is part of the thirty year story of Peter Dominic, and the first part of this book describes some of the events which led to the success of them both. Readers bored rigid by the history of commercial companies are cordially advised to skip both Part I and the brief notes below, turning to the entertaining articles by many contributors in the other three parts of the book.

In his flattering Foreword, André Simon describes how Paul Dauthieu, a Scot of French parents settled in Scotland, began with one shop in Horsham in 1939, just as the war had begun. In 1963, when the business was sold to International Distillers and Vintners for three quarters of a million pounds, the one shop had become twenty. Then in 1968, Paul Dauthieu died of cancer on the eve of retiring.

Having weathered the war, thanks in no small measure to his wife, Blanche, who ran the shop with a growing team of women while her husband was in the R.A.F., Paul had managed by 1956 to add another nine branches, all in good Southern market towns. This was no mean achievement; applications for licences were almost always opposed by competitors, often successfully, and with whisky rationed, Peter Dominic—non-existent before the war— received an inadequate quota of the leading brands.

With wine, the company was more fortunate. A chance association (see Ordinary Fun in the Fifties) led to Henri Lemaire in Bordeaux and the shipping of his three Vins Ordinaires now so well known as 'Carafino'. Joining the firm in 1956, I remember being most impressed with these wines; they were so much smoother than any 'Ordinaires' I had drunk in France. That Lemaire was pioneering a new technique of quicker maturing by refrigeration (later to be widely adopted for cheap wines) was unknown to me. Not that this mattered, I liked these wines and, apart from any business considerations, felt I would be doing wine drinkers a service by publicising them.

Thus began *Peter Dominic's Wineyard* in the Epicure columns, which The Times and other comparable papers had just started. Having described Vin Ordinaire in light hearted fashion (is there any other way of doing it?) we moved in similar vein to other wines, blossoming forth too with as many leaflets as time permitted, including an apology for a newspaper called 'The Daily Quaff (Forward with the Bottle)'.

It was only a matter of time before the blossom turned to fruit and in 1959 out came the first WINEMINE ('A Mine of Wine Information') just—but only just—in time for Christmas. After the Editor, Art Editor and printers' names, Paul Dauthieu added:

'The team being inspired and instructed, enraged, cajoled, harried and delayed by The Boss—who also paid.'

He had an extraordinary gift of transforming irritation and frustration in subordinates into a grin of endearment, an even better example being his habit of saying, 'You've got to remember that all bosses are bastards,' whenever this was precisely what you *were* thinking.

Since 1968 when International Distillers and Vintners' three hundred and fifty branches were merged under one name—Peter Dominic, the average print order for each WINEMINE, (Summer and Winter) has exceeded 150,000 copies. Nobody pretends they are all sold at 2s each; regular customers receive one free and rightly so.

This then, is the background of what I have perhaps optimistically called 'A First Anthology', taken almost entirely from the years 1960 to 1965, facts and figures being brought up to date. I begin it with a memory, 'Ordinary Fun in the Fifties', partly because these were stirring times for me and my colleagues, leading to WINEMINE, and partly because with brands of Ordinaires now being launched almost weekly, some future archivist may want to know about the first.

ACKNOWLEDGEMENTS

If the success of Peter Dominic first led to WINEMINE, the willingness of other writers to contribute—some members of the Circle of Wine Writers, others even more distinguished men of letters—has been the prime factor ensuring its success. I record my thanks to them, particularly to those who have allowed me to reproduce their articles here.

I am particularly indebted to Monsieur André Simon for writing the Foreword when 93 and almost blind. Offering him any chronological help he might need, I shall always remember his voice on the telephone, clear as champagne, saying, 'Of course I remember how you joined the wine trade; it was because *I* said, "Paul, *you* can't w-r-r-ite!"'

Design and layout, without which WINEMINE would have been still born, have been undertaken throughout by the David Paul Design Group of Chichester; my thanks go to David Goodman, Rodney Symes and others of the group, aided so often when good photographs were lacking, by Guy Gravett, best known as Glyndebourne's official photographer.

Would that I commanded the entire cellars of Peter Dominic—lock, stock and barrel—from which to remunerate all contributors! Yet, as well perhaps that I do not, lest the firm be broke and the contributors incapable.

WineMine
A First Anthology

PART ONE

The Dominic Story
by Anthony Hogg

PETER DOMINIC

Carafino

ROSÉ

Miss Pitcher 1965

Ordinary Fun in the Fifties

There is nothing earth shaking about exchange visits between French and English young people, yet it was thanks to one of them that thousands of gallons of Carafino wines are now being drunk daily in Britain.

It all began with a small classified advertisement in a French newspaper to the effect that a Horsham family wished to arrange an exchange for their daughter of eighteen. When, soon afterwards, Paula Dauthieu went out to Bordeaux and later Hubert Lemaire came to Horsham, the preceding exchange of correspondence between their parents had established that at least neither would be homesick for lack of wine. Paula's father was head of Peter Dominic; Hubert's was head of Lemaire et Cie in Bordeaux, négociants who specialised in Vins Ordinaires on a large scale.

The result, in 1952, was *Big Value in Big Bottles*. Behind the slogan there was feverish activity at Horsham. Every empty Vermouth bottle was being eagerly seized for the reception of Lemaire's three Ordinaires—Rouge, Rosé and Blanc. A washing machine worked by the 'United Nations'—a team of one-time refugee ladies of many nationalities—emitted as much steam as Stephenson's Rocket yet without fatal casualties, or the precaution of a red flag flown at the bottling line near by. Surprisingly it emitted clean bottles too.

The advantages of the larger bottles—and later to an even greater extent of gallon and half gallon jars—were that less corks and labels were needed per hogshead, to say nothing of time and labour saved when bottling it. The saving—no more than a few pence per bottle perhaps—was nevertheless large enough for the consumer to appreciate. The simplest labels in black and white proclaimed merely, 'Vin Ordinaire', which came to be translated in greatly addicted circles as 'Dominic's Plonk'. (An Australian trade acquaintance was deeply shocked at this irreverence.)

By 1957, the time had come to advertise. But how? there was little money to spare for this. Luckily *The Times* and the 'top' Sunday papers were just starting epicure columns at reduced rates. But what could we say week after week about 'Plonk'? It was not Château Lafite!

This largely explains why the weekly *Peter Dominic's Wineyard* said almost anything that entered our heads. Surprisingly the readers never demanded that these should be examined; they wrote for a 'Trial Three' instead. Our search through books and magazines for copy inspiration became as desperate as the one for empty Vermouth bottles. Tennyson gave us to think that the young Lord Lover was really being 'stood up' at the garden gate at least until Maud had drained the last drop of Vin Rosé. Disraeli's Mr Mountchesney, who only liked bad wine, was a source of inspiration; there were Big *Bad* Bottles that week! One fashion paper was not amused by 'waist hugging little labels . . . and corks in rissole beige worn right into the neck', but there was no 'come-back' from the astrologers—perhaps 'What the Jars Foretell' was no more accurate than the stars' predictions.

The origin of Pollard was an architect who built a church but forgot the altar. Pollard, who suffered from 'Wine Starvation', merely forgot the staircase but was later (thanks to Vin Ordinaire) awarded a bronze medal for his revolutionary design with three staircases in a one-storey building.

With characters like the brilliant Pollard

13

and the influential City magnate Sir 'Alf A' Gallon joining the Rouge, Rosé and Blanc colours, Dominic's Own Vin Ordinaire Drinkers (the DOVODs) had become such a fashionable regiment that Lord Lapper-Litre volunteered to become Colonel-in-chief, even though he declared he had never heard a bottle drunk in anger.

But DOVOD recruits were not wholly fictitious; Gilbert Harding was large as life and only too real. His 24s 6d postal order for a Trial Three appeared one day in the post. Since he lived near our Brighton branch, we sent a boy round with the parcel and 1s 4d change, which was a part postage charge. Gilbert was astonished. He telephoned to ask whether he could come to Horsham to find out who these extraordinary people were who returned him 1s 4d. The outcome was the first of several lunch parties and his apparent devotion to Dominic for what remained of his life.

Keeping enough of the Ordinaires in 'the pipe line' between Bordeaux and Horsham was always a problem with such rapidly growing demand. One Saturday, towards the end of November 1959, we foresaw a Christmas crisis unless a further supply could be bottled and distributed within fourteen days. To his eternal credit, the Commercial Manager of Silver City Airways was in his Southampton office when we telephoned that Saturday afternoon. By Tuesday, forty hogsheads had left Bordeaux by road for Cherbourg; on Thursday they were being unloaded from Silver City Bristol freighters at Southampton Airport. This well executed—but hardly profitable—combined operation finally secured the DOVOD supply lines that year.

By 1962, our nameless wonders needed a protected name. 'Carafino' hardly sounds French, but at that time Bordeaux prices were rising so rapidly it seemed we might have to look to Italy or Spain for your (and indeed our) daily drinking. The crisis passed; Lemaire have continued to ship the three wines from Bordeaux, not in 48-gallon hogsheads for they have long since been superceded by 'maritime' metal containers each holding 540 gallons.

Bards and Beetles

QUESTION FROM JOHN BARR OF CARNOUSTIE

I seem to remember I read in 'The Mine',
A poem of praise of the Florentine wine
In Siennese cellars each bottle is numbered
But your shipper has slipped or his cellarman slumbered.

My flask of Chianti—Gallo Nero Riserva
Contained a black beetle—bene preserva
The body I send you for closest inspection
(The head I discarded at time of detection).

I know that in Liverpool beetles are fine
But I really don't fancy them pickled in wine.
To guests I was singing good Dominic's praises
When out floats this monster; a question it raises—

Now bad Peter Dominic taken to task
Just how did this beetle get into that flask?

Readers are asked not to conclude from these two pages that serious complaints are treated with levity by Peter Dominic. There was 'screaming hysteria' over this one from Carnoustie to Siena at the time!

ANSWER FROM ROBERT GITTINGS

The Duke of Wellington was asked a question
Concerning rats once found in Spanish bottles;
The lady who enquired made the suggestion
These were young rats crept in to wet their throttles.

'No, ma'am,' replied the Duke, in accents martial,
'Very large rats!' The lady grew uncertain:
'Enormous bottles, then?' With air impartial,
'No,' said the Duke, 'Very small bottles'! Curtain.

Some such complete and militant non sequitur
I'd like to find about this blessed beetle.
Alas, the Duke is dead; I'm no executor
Of his terse utterance and his logic lethal.

But this I'll say (regretting though the reason)
Beetles mean luck, whatever shape or size, sir.
This was, perhaps, a compliment of the season.
The bottle with the beetle wins a prize, sir!

Leading Sparkler

If Vin Ordinaire (subsequently Carafino) played the lead in the successful run of Peter Dominic, the sparkling white burgundy called Cristal Dry was a pretty strong supporter. Until the mid fifties, with few exceptions, retail wine merchants bought their wines from the shippers in London, who were the British agents for 'their principals' abroad. The system worked well in the days when the wine drinking public was largely limited to the upper middle classes and their butlers, but as a wider, more cost-conscious section of people took to wine, enterprising retailers began to cut out the middle-man and new names and new wines appeared.

It must be difficult for the public to understand how new shippers' names can still appear on labels when our trade with the Continent has been going so long that 'the lot' should have been seen by now. The explanation is that in most districts, Burgundy being a particularly good example, there are hundreds and hundreds of vineyard owner/producers, the great majority being quite content to sell their wines to their own countrymen. The few, who do export, perhaps began when a member of the family married a foreigner which led to suitable contacts, but usually the initiative has come from a foreign buyer, speaking their language in order to convince them that exporting would be profitable.

With his French, his experience of the Trade and shrewd observation of the widening interest in wine as our Welfare State got into its post-war stride, Paul Dauthieu was perfectly equipped to establish direct contacts abroad whence new wines could be shipped exclusively to Peter Dominic. One of these was the small family firm of Meulien Pigneret, specialists in sparkling white burgundy in Rully, at the southern end of the district. The result of his first visit became 'Cristal Dry'.

Although I had become quite a knowledgeable amateur in the decade after the war, I had never heard of sparkling white burgundy until, in 1955 visiting Bouchard Père et Fils at Beaune, I was given a sparkling aperitif, which I took to be Champagne. They smiled, pleased no doubt at a guest's thoughts which flattered. For the fact is that handed a glass of sparkling wine, nearly everybody assumes it is champagne, drinking it happily, unless some hint is given that it is not.

Later came the realisation that any father bold enough to depart from convention by serving sparkling white burgundy (then 17s 6d a bottle) at a wedding reception instead of champagne (then 23s 6d a bottle) could make a considerable saving to put in his own pocket or to pass on to his daughter if he felt rich enough.

This was a bull point for Cristal Dry, carefully explained in a leaflet, which any parents rash enough to put their postal address in The Times Engagement columns duly received. At a time when there were few books on wine and the most popular one, Raymond Postgate's *Plain Man's Guide,* published in 1951, did not even mention sparkling white burgundy, it was surprising how quickly Cristal Dry became 'The Wine for Launching the Bride'.

Among the first to embark on the voyage of discovery was a retired Admiral in Sussex and I rather think there have been a good many Cristal Dry weddings in the family by now. Far from being invented, the following in the first WINEMINE merely told the truth:

Cristal Dry has not yet launched a thousand ships, but it has launched many a Helen down the slipway into the ocean of connubial bliss! One such 'Helen' was the sister of a midshipman, whose aunt promptly ordered it for the midshipman's cousin's wedding. Perhaps we may now anticipate the marriage of the Midshipman himself—on the quarterdeck of H.M.S. Pinafore—

For he holds that Cristal Dry,
That wine from Burgundy,
A matrimonious harmonious tone implants;
And so do his sisters and his cousins and his
*   aunts;*
His sisters and his cousins—
They just order it in dozens—
And his aunts!

After this, it was difficult to find anything witty to say, but naval associations helped once again with the 'flimsy', the chit given to every officer at the end of each appointment which has to be a précis of his confidential report. Leading Sparkler Cristal Dry was proud to publish two of hers. (In real naval life the classic flimsy was always said to be one which read—after a two year commission—'I have seen this officer sober, not once, not twice, but *three* times'.)

After a strip cartoon illustrating Mrs Ffoulkes-Ffotheringay's fashionable champagne party where only 'Mr Dominic' realised the wine was not champagne and 'A new experience for Virgo' predicted by the clairvoyante, 'Gazing into the famous Cristal (Dry)', Mary Priestley did the charming Tinker Tailor drawings illustrated on page 20. The duplicated leaflet then became a 12-page wedding brochure, with an aide-mémoire on who pays for what (the bell-ringers, the buttonholes and so on) kindly checked by a clergyman in Sutton.

Cost apart, there is much to be said for sparkling wines at wedding receptions. Many

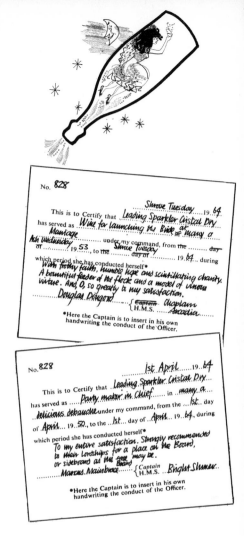

Confidential Reports on Cristal Dry

are a little sweeter than the dry Champagnes shipped to the British market, making them better suited to wedding cake, certainly at 3pm in a hot marquee. Popularity of sparkling wines has increased steadily in the past decade, Cristal Dry giving ground to Aimé Boucher's cheaper Sparkling Vouvray as far as WINEMINE's list is concerned.

But for my 'Leading Sparkler' that made a few wedding days less costly for his sisters and his cousins and his aunts I shall always hold a special affection.

Tinker Tailor 1863

Soldier brave   Sailor true   Skilled Physician   Varsity blue

Portly Rector   Squire so hale   Crafty Lawyer   Curate pale

Tinker Tailor 1963

Moët Chandon   L. Lebon   Cristal Dry   or Jacquesson

Lanson, Heidsieck   Vintage Krug   Ordinaire served from
a Jug!

Orange Street about 1870.
The 'Old Tennis Court' was
on the first floor.

Tastings and Fairs

One wet winter evening in 1958, driving from Horsham to attend a Peter Dominic tasting in the Assembly Hall at Worthing, Paul Dauthieu announced that he thought he had obtained the lease of some cellars in London. For me— recently promoted 'Mail Order Manager' after two years with Peter Dominic, it was an exciting possibility. However great their enthusiasm for our Vin Ordinaire, Londoners could hardly be expected to order their supplies from the small country town of Horsham 40 miles away. A London retail shop was a necessity and this is what the old vaults at 2-8 Orange Street, off the Haymarket became.

Orange Street, running east from by the Haymarket Theatre into the Charing Cross Road by the Garrick, dates from 1905. Before this time, the Haymarket end was James Street, the middle part Blue Cross Street and the Charing Cross end Orange Street. James and Blue Cross Streets date from about 1673 when Samuel Pepys was 'dining very handsomely' at the Cock in Suffolk Street round the corner, or walking from Pall Mall to Coventry Street between the hedges of 'Hedge Lane'.

TENNIS TO TASTINGS

The history of these vaults is much older. Since the Tudors, real tennis had been very much the Royal game, though one wonders how mobile Henry VIII might have been. There were several courts in the West end, including one in Windmill Street, which perhaps never closed like the theatre there in World War II. Another court, above these Orange Street vaults, seems to have been a going concern before 1660 when the name of Colonel Panton (Panton Street) first appears in the records.

The Tennis court was probably part of a celebrated gaming house established in 1635, spoken of by Lord Clarendon in his History of the Rebellion as 'A fair house for entertainment and gaming with handsome gravel walks with shade, and where were an upper and lower bowling green whither very many of the nobility and gentry of the best quality resorted, both for exercise and conversation.'

Neither bowling nor bingo being in our line, we have since tried to maintain tradition by means of the Wine Mine Club, where the wines certainly are 'of the best quality', and if the members are not all to be found in Debrett, they certainly resort for conversation and the healthy exercise of lifting the elbow.

In the eighteenth century, tennis went out of fashion and the building became Punch's Theatre in 1737, with a second theatre (The New) added in 1741. But in 1780 tennis revived and, as still inscribed on the facade, 'The Old Tennis Court' became headquarters of the game until 1886. When the Court was dismantled, the benches of the *dedans* went to the Merton Street Court at Oxford and the stone floor to Warwick Castle but the stones were too worn for further use. The vaults seem

OSMER SHEPHERD

BUSHERS

COACH
FACTORY

Orange Street circa 1870

Tony Hancock at one of the earlier Peter Dominic Tastings

to have been occupied by wine merchants without a break since 1815.

'Are you sure Henry VIII didn't have a game of tennis with one of those wives and a noggin down here afterwards?' Monty Modling asked me recently, before embarking on a hilarious tasting for Thames Television.

'I fear we can't claim that', I said.

We had just walked from Covent Garden, with every porter stopping work and shouting 'Wotcher Monty!' as he recognised the celebrity.

There was no need to have worried about Henry VIII. After seeing the programme, it was obvious that one live Cockney comedian was far better for 2-8 Orange Street than a dead Monarch and all his wives.

THE WINEMINE CLUB

The problem, having acquired 2-8 Orange Street and fitted it out as a retail shop, was to make the place known. It was only a cellar, reached from the street by a forbiddingly steep ladder; there was no shop window and although everybody knows the Haymarket, those acquainted with Orange Street were likely to be limited to visitors to Constable, the publisher, and to regular buyers of caviare. (When W. G. White, the caviare merchants, moved to Dean Street that left only the writers and who pays them enough money to buy wine!)

The solution was The Wine Mine Club offering regular tastings of wines to members upon payment. This was something new; wine merchants often hired halls, giving parties where their cheapest wines would be on sample, but none had taken the matter a stage further, offering fine wines—a range of clarets for example—to give the public the same chances of comparing wines as the Trade enjoyed.

In starting the Wine Mine Club, Paul Dauthieu was, I think, encouraged by the success of the Wine and Food Society's lunches and dinners, which were being well attended in the provinces as well as in London. He had, incidentally, the highest regard for André Simon, the kindest of men, who had befriended him between the wars in London when Paul, starting from nothing, had worked his way up from a commis waiter at Claridges to the valued representative of Grierson Oldham, supplying wines to the Savoy and other fashionable places.

Although born and bred in the Highlands, Paul's parents were as French as André himself; thus both were Frenchmen struggling at times in the same trade. André Simon, losing his job as a shipper in the 1931 crisis, started the Wine and Food Society. Paul Dauthieu, asked to take half salary when the war began in 1939, started his own business.

The success of the Wine Mine Club seemed fairly certain. Ever since the first WINEMINE, the recurring theme of readers' letters had been, 'If only I had the money, I would like to try them all'. So, in 1960, the business began of trying at least some of them, which has now led to all of them in turn. Eight hundred people —sixty at a time—paid 10s a head to taste and compare 1953 and 1955 clarets and another seven hundred paid 15s for ten wines from the Riesling grape, prices including buffet, more table wine, something post-prandial and a hard seat (if you were lucky) on a case of claret.

The following year the Club settled to its now familiar pattern of five meetings each year, demand for tickets exceeding supply until 1968 when some members, not surprisingly, became temporarily shaken by the risen cost of wine due principally to successive increases on duty. Having advertised Orange Street as 'A mashie shot from Piccadilly Circus and only a putt from Burberry's new golf school', we were too busy the first year keeping our eye on the glass to lift our head and notice the members. But in 1961, WINEMINE reported:

No diploma in Social Science is needed to tell you that there are many ways in which 65 people attending a Tasting in a wine merchant's cellar could be classified. Males, females, over 40, under 40, accents (Eton or Borstal) or indeed, attitudes while tasting. The attitudes provide a fine field for research; 'The Dog and Bone' (nose completely buried in glass); 'The Bad Smell-on-the-Waistcoat' (complaint likely any moment) and others, but to give you some idea of the members of the Wine Mine Club we shall classify them by hats. (See over).

The Wine Mine Club.

GUY GRAVETT

29

The Wine Mine Club.

MEN	
Deerstalkers	1
Bowlers, and of course rolled up umbrellas	7
A. Edens, and of course rolled up umbrellas	4
Battered Homburgs	9
Cloth Caps	3
Possible heirloom of M. Chevalier	1
Crash Helmet	1
Letting down Lincoln Bennett	14
	—
	40
	—

WOMEN	
Possible heirloom of the late Queen Victoria	1
Seen in Vogue or Harpers	4
Seen in Women's Own	7
Home made from an idea in "The Birdwatcher"	1
Felt; but far better unseen	2
Letting down the 'she-paper' advertisers	10
	—
	25
	—

Knowledge of wine—like the hats—varies from member to member. A rich 'bowler' may be deciding which wines he will lay down; an 'A. Eden' brings his son along for a little vinous education, still not provided by our great Public schools in spite of the fees; the 'battered Homburgs' succumbed perhaps to the charms of France and Italy during the War, returning on holiday every year since, while the cloth cap in the corner, soulfully looking at a case of Richebourg, turns out to be half a Frenchman anyway, who after 50 years in London will never be reconciled to milk or beer.

Three years later the members themselves wrote on 'My Kind of Night Club', pride of place being given to J. C. Haydon of Shoreham, who had not missed one of the twenty-three meetings. '*My* kind of Night Club puts on *lunch time* sessions!' he wrote.

T. R. Gilbert, a London bank official in his fifties, neatly provided the recipe for the Club itself:

'Take a dozen different wines, related to one another by their species, or by nationality, or by their distinction: then take a dozen people of both sexes, who are related by the same love of wine . . . Mix well and the result is *my* kind of Night Club.'

While Colin Davies, put the Club to a hospitable use which WINEMINE was convinced would lead to his own rapid promotion.

Colin Davies, a young Redhill advertising executive, awaits yet another 'starchy' client on the platform at King's Cross. What is to be done for his entertainment this time? Shakespeare? The Mermaid? Finchley's new Italian Restaurant? He remembers a friend who had two spare tickets for The WINE MINE CLUB. A telephone call and all is fixed. They will be waiting for him at the Dominic door.

Dinner on the Pullman has made the North-country client even 'starchier' than usual, so an entertainment involving a lift of the elbow and at least a pace or two between samples is well received. Avoiding (so *they* think!) the Dominic eye of disapproval, they skip the lesser wines and soon find a common topic of interest in how to get three glasses of the best without being noticed. By now the general atmosphere is animated. ('Who would have thought that large lady would be seen talking to that emaciated Vicar?') In spite of the Pullman, the North-country guest is now ready for the Buffet and finds the Horsham bread even better than 'oop North. It's yet more starch of course, but now it doesn't really matter; liquified by those three glasses of Château-bottled, it could hardly restore the original stiff front.

On the way to the hotel, the guest plans his next London visit to coincide with the Champagne Tasting. And, in Dominics we feel sure that Mr. Davies is now handling the biggest account of his career and designing one of those advertisements which ends—'Thinks —"Thanks to the WINE MINE CLUB."'

MAY DAYS WITH MONOPOLE
Another feature of The Wine Mine Club—memorable for all but particularly for one guest who missed the plane back and for another who fell in the champagne vat—has been the annual outing we call 'May Days with Monopole'.

May Days with Monopole. Clement Freud is the speaker.

The Chelsea Wine Fair. Richard Boon, General Manager, explains the Fun of the Fair to Vice-Admiral and Mrs Durnford (Mayor and Mayoress of Chelsea).

34

Some sixty members rise at an hour when even grape addicts can only face strong black coffee, in order to fly for a day in Reims, where they are the guests of Heidsieck Monopole. Then towards dusk, they climb back into the plane in a far higher state of morale than they were at dawn, yet needing black coffee once more.

Henri Chapman and Henri Visser, directors of Heidsieck D. M., like most Champagne shippers believe in entertaining properly. Rodney Symes, art editor of WINEMINE, went along one year to take photographs. After the tour of the cellars, the mid-morning glass, the sumptuous lunch and travelling around betweenwhiles in motor-coaches with police outriders, he felt happy but tired when the members took off for home, leaving him behind (purposely!) to spend the next day with his camera quietly in the vineyards.

'It wasn't till they'd gone that the party really began,' he still says incredulously.

'There were the people at the Airport—the customs, the dolly guides, the coach drivers and the police motorcyclists. They all had to have champagne. What a day! But it was nothing to the night!'

50TH MEETING

In the spring of this year Orange Street celebrated the fiftieth meeting with a tasting of clarets of the 1950 decade. 50 meetings with 600/650 people and a dozen wines on sample at each! I think that makes about 400,000 glasses washed up. When you have a place associated with Charles I, tradition has to be maintained. They still pass a chain of buckets up the cellar.

THE CHELSEA WINE FAIRS

To a Sussex firm like Peter Dominic, the county in 1961 seemed full of the pioneering spirit. In Chichester, Powell and Moya were knocking up the Festival Theatre as fast as the sixpences poured in to pay for it. Owners of ancestral homes were planning to lure the fashionable world on summer Saturday nights to *Concertos Grosso* and alfresco suppers with wine, at five guineas a munch. Fanned by these cultural breezes blowing round the county from Glyndebourne, it was time for Peter Dominic to arrange some further, if meaner, beauty of the night; and London, which had every show except a Wine Show, seemed by far the safest place.

Following the established precept of making the guests pay, there were at the first Chelsea Wine Fair, some 300 wines from 14 countries on sample at 6d a tasting glass. This charge, on top of an entrance fee of 7s 6d, occasioned some surprise in the Press, but the Fair was being held for people genuinely interested in wine, as opposed to those who merely wanted an evening's cheap drinking, of which Chelsea can doubtless claim a fair share.

The decision was wise. To the surprise of the Town Hall officials (except the 'chuckers-out' who were unemployed and disappointed) there were no incidents. On the financial side, the loss was less than the experts had predicted. 6d a glass just about paid for the wine drunk but 7s 6d a head by no means covered the main expenses, such as hire of hall, advertising, making the stands, and board and lodging in London for some fifty members of the Dominic staff.

The Fair was held for three days during the Motor Show from noon to 3pm and 6 to 9pm daily. Every evening the Town Hall—whose capacity was only 700—became too crowded, though the visitors—long trained on roads and in commuters' trains—appeared quite unconcerned. At midday, the Hall was barely half full with not a few visitors turning out to be buyers from the wine departments of Breweries, educating themselves on Château Latour at 6d a glass. (And the report ended prophetically for so many with: They'll be taking us all over tomorrow so we must have our quip today!)

The verses of Arthur Hugh Clough (1819–1861), Le Diner (in The Oxford Book of Light Verse) might have been written to illustrate the photographs of the Fair which WINEMINE published.

The following year (1962), the Fair ran for four nights, again at The Chelsea Town Hall, with all tickets (700 a night) sold in advance. Hearing from an old friend, Donald Tweddell, that he was to be the organiser of the U.K.

36

Some well known personalities at the Chelsea Wine Fair.

See more... Savour more... Sip more...

ALL THE WORLD'S WINES
ON SAMPLE AT 6d A GLASS

at the Chelsea

WINE FAIR

Promoted—not Pensioned—to

THE SEYMOUR HALL

LONDON W.I.

22-26 OCTOBER, 1963.

Noon to 3.0 p.m. and 5.30 to 9.0 p.m. Daily

Tickets **7/6** each

GRAND TRAFALGAR DAY FORETASTE
in aid of
KING GEORGE'S FUND FOR SAILORS

Monday 21st October 6 p.m.   Tickets One Guinea

Freedom from Hunger Campaign (nobody had heard of this at the time) I persuaded my colleagues to hold 'a Foretaste' in aid of it, though I had no idea whether the result would be £5 or £500.

In the organisation of our three Fairs, Richard Boon (now a wine merchant in his own right in Stourbridge) was the 'outside' man, whose job was to fill the hall with exhibitors, staff, stands and bottles; mine was to fill it with people—the more important the better—to taste them. Even had there been the money, I think we would have scorned professional P.R. assistance, but I do remember we engaged an amateur of P.R. She came to lunch, her scent being so powerful that nobody could smell the wine. By the opening night, she had become so keen about wine that Château Latour appeared to have ousted Chanel altogether.

If the P.R. lady was something of a disappointment, so were the V.I.P.'s connected with the United Nations Association. None accepted our invitation. From my desk in Horsham hundreds of invitations went out to celebrities, but to me, hoping to justify my own idea, the results were disappointing; with one exception. Gerald Moore wrote applauding our enterprise, and I felt at the time that the cheque for £5 in the envelope was as great as any of his better known accompaniments.

Support rarely comes, as innocents may learn, from expected quarters. It was not the famous but the Dominic customers—the members of the Wine Mine Club, the Vin Ordinaire addicts, just the drinkers if you like—who rallied to the cause. By paying 2 guineas for Foretaste tickets, they contributed the bulk of the £260 we gave to Freedom from Hunger. The other £30 came from the campaign boxes in the hall—2s a head from about 300 Press and celebrities! And that after tasting 300 wines 'on the House'!

On the night endeavour was rewarded.

The Daily Sketch next morning carried pictures of two Chancellors of the Exchequer—The Chancellor Reginald Maudling and his Labour 'shadow' Harold Wilson—sampling wine at the Fair. Whether or not they put 2s in the campaign box, Peter Dominic's £261, which appeared in the first list of contributions, did its bit for Freedom from Hunger.

AND STILL MORE

The capacity of the Seymour Hall, booked for 1963 to avoid the congestion of Chelsea, was held to be 2000 against 700. But when twenty shippers and half a dozen countries decided to project their lovely images with tastefully decorated stands by the cubit, it began to look as if the tasters would be little better off for elbow room than they were before.

In the event, 1500 people were there each evening, all apparently skilled in holding a glass, a programme and a sample of cheese at one and the same time. (Some Heath Robinson needs to design a shooting stick with attachments to hold all the accoutrements of Wine Tasting.)

These three Chelsea Wine Fairs, so efficiently run by Richard Boon and staffed by almost the whole company brought to London from our twenty shops, were the climax of Peter Dominic as a privately owned independent family firm. The agreement with International Distillers and Vintners was signed almost immediately afterwards. Doubtless the Fairs would have continued in favourable conditions, but with the ending of retail price maintenance, the stability of the wine trade was undermined, bringing a host of new problems as one private company after another sought shelter from the storm of price cutting under the umbrellas of bigger concerns.

As a sailor might say, Peter Dominic, as a private ship, had had a memorable first commission.

WineMine
A First Anthology

PART TWO

WineMine at Home

Some Tots and Sips

by J. B. Priestley

Illustrated by his daughter, Mary Priestley

Let us begin with the arts, not the drinks. Now a lot of nice people, who want to appreciate books, pictures, music, soon run into difficulties. They do not know, chiefly because nobody has told them, that we must still suit our own tastes on every level. So-and-so may be a man of genius, but that does not mean he is the man of genius we want. We simply may not be able to get along with him. His work is good, perhaps it is great, but we cannot put ourselves in sympathy with it. And failure to understand that personal tastes still operate on these high levels, that we cannot be expected to enjoy everything, has made —and is still making—a lot of nice people miserable.

It is the same with our drink. Too many people, once they have left the bottled beer, gin-and-it, whisky-and-splash, low level, and are beginning to look through wine lists, imagine they ought to be able to enjoy everything. But generally they can't. And apart from any niceties of the palate, there are often sound physical reasons, probably to do with the functioning of the liver and kidneys, why they can't.

Here I can write with some feeling. In the matter of wine-drinking, my palate and my interior functioning have long been at war. For I enjoy above all wines the noble white Burgundies, and next to them any fine Hocks. I have not only a taste but a kind of imaginative sympathy for such wines. But—by some irony —these are the very wines my body, as distinct from my mind, cannot cope with. I could sip a glass without any risk but I am by temperament no glass-sipper, being eager and greedy, demanding an ample supply of what I like or none at all. Yes, I *can* do without, gladly pouring out wines for our guests without taking anything but a preliminary tasting sip for myself.

As a mind I am far happier with wines, which have more to offer the imagination, than I am with spirits. As a body—and an ageing one at that—I am now more at ease with spirits. I have sometimes thought that people, physically not mentally, can be divided quite sharply into Mediterranean and Baltic types. The Mediterranean type can drink any amount of wine without any ill effects. These lucky people can spend weeks in France, tippling away, and come back looking fresh and rosy. But if I go there and am unable to resist temptation, within four days I have dark bags under my eyes and look like a gangster night-club owner

THE MEDITERRANEAN

42

in a film. My metabolism—alas—is not Mediterranean but Baltic.

This means that within reasonable limits I can enjoy without such ill effects the powerful distillations of the North—the whiskies (including the pale but potent Malts), the schnappses, the vodkas, of which there are more varieties than can be found here. All these, which most Mediterranean types approach with dread, I can drink with pleasure. But I take care to follow the Baltic practice of always eating something with them, not a meal, little things fairly rich in fats. These strong spirits were never intended to be poured into empty stomachs. And I would include among such drinks all the powerful dry martinis, the Gibsons, the Montgomerys, and the rest. They should be taken with canapés. I have noticed during the last ten years that the dry martini, once its mainstay, has almost been banished from the New York cocktail party. Nearly everybody drinks tall, weak, over-iced highballs. I think the dry martini—a great American contribution to world civilisation—should be brought back, but with plenty of fatty little things pressed on to the guests.

I have done a lot of travelling in my time. During most of my travels I have followed the sensible old custom of drinking the wines and spirits of the country. What the local people prefer is generally something that suits the atmosphere and climate of the place. What originally came out of the regional soil helps one to enjoy the region. But not always of course, especially if one has gone a long way from home. Some local brews and distillations in exotic places are best left alone. But I learnt to enjoy Tequila in Mexico and Pisco in Chile. And, though this is being treacherous to our export trade, I must confess that when I am in America now, I rarely drink the imported Scotch, greatly preferring America's own whisky—Bourbon. The fine old Bourbons— and the best I have ever had is Jack Daniels' Black Label—are really magnificent whiskies,

which may be given a little water but no soda, no ginger ale, no nonsense.

What I avoid, unless the worst comes to the worst, are those faraway brews and distillations that are bad imitations of good originals elsewhere. Oriental whiskies, for example, with labels looking like a parade of Argyll and Sutherland Highlanders. Or those tremendously 'London' gins concocted and bottled at least seven hundred miles from Bow Bells. On the other hand, though the very best brandies come from France, I have had good brandies that originated elsewhere. When I was in the Soviet Union many years ago, I much enjoyed their brandy which came, I think, from Armenia; it was like good Armagnac.

In places as distant and far apart as South Australia and California I have drunk daily some excellent local wines. The mistake that has been made in such places has nothing to do with the quality of the wines, but has much to do with the naming of them. Names like *Claret* and *Burgundy* and *Hock* should never have been adopted; they encourage comparisons that are better not made; while at the same time the genuine and original qualities of these wines, Australian or African, American or Chilean, may easily be ignored. There is something appealing to me in the idea of these men (generally French or Italian) who went to far distant places, almost to the ends of the earth, to begin cultivating the vine, to press new but still enchanted grapes. They were spreading civilisation.

Inability to drink white wines (which are more acid than red) as one grows older is not uncommon. I speak from personal experience, believing that had I trained my system more on wine and less on spirits all might still be well. The moral for young people wishing to enjoy wine into their nineties, like M. André Simon, is to keep to the grape and if you smoke, do so on a full stomach. Editor

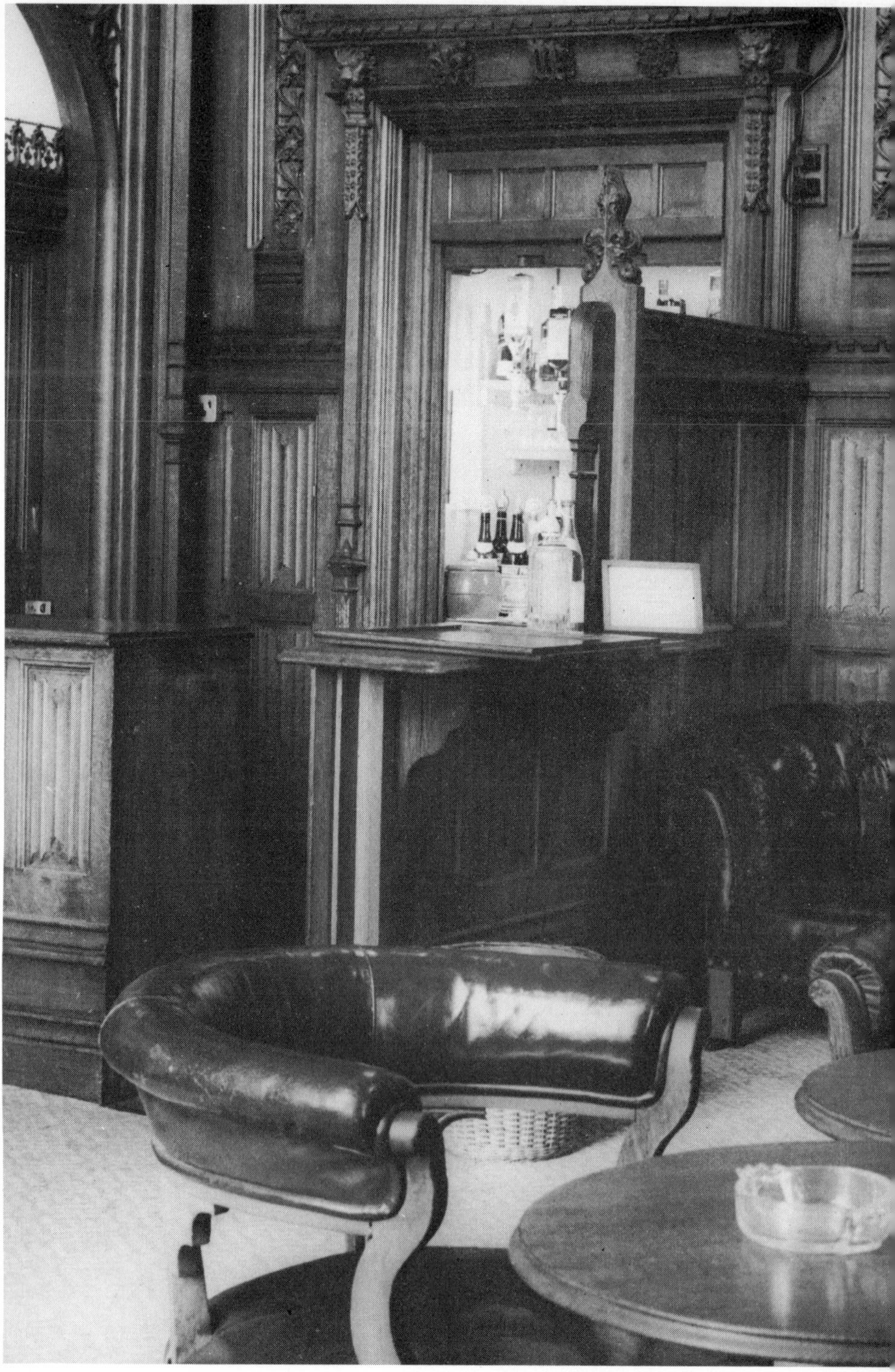

The Members' Smokeroom

The Bars
of The House

by Trevor Lloyd-Hughes

Chief Information Adviser to H.M. Government, 1965–1970, Trevor Lloyd-Hughes contributed this article in 1964, when he had been a political journalist at Westminster for many years. The bar that disappeared has re-appeared; this, and other changes, he describes in a footnote.

The House of Commons is most uncommon when it comes to drinking—as it does to the tune of some 35,000 bottles a year, not counting beer. Most of this flows down the throats not of our legislators, but of their guests.

Because Westminster is a Royal Palace, the ordinary licensing laws, and hours, do not apply. In fact, the Queen's Pub, as someone dubbed it, is open so long as Parliament is sitting.

Seven bars are supplied from quaint and far from ideal cellars under the building, alongside the Thames. The Stranger's Bar, once called the Illegal Bar, where you could be bought a drink by your M.P.; the Press Bar, in the quarters of the Parliamentary journalists, a flourishing corner of the whole labyrinth where the acoustics are so dreadful that it is easier to contemplate the Spy cartoons of former politicians than to try to talk; and five other bars, including one in the M.P.s' Smoke Room.

One bar has disappeared.* Known for many years as 'Annie's Bar' (Annie was a big, red and very popular barmaid' it was mainly for M.P.s in a small room off the Members' Lobby, now used much more drearily as an

Annie's Bar

Opposition Whips' office. Here Victoriana ran riot, in the shape of sandwiches under domes of glass, an ancient coffee machine and marble-topped tables.

The Commons cellar *is* striking—literally. Tall men need to duck under low-slung lines of water pipes that clutter the ceiling and help to maintain a cosy but unsuitable temperature nigh on 70 degrees Fahrenheit, despite the efforts of the Refreshment Department Manager, Mr. E. G. Roberts, who has had all the hot pipes insulated. One intriguing oddment is an alcove packed with porous pot pipes that can hold wine bottles. This honeycomb contraption used to be used as a kind of refrigerator, by running cold water over it. It worked!

Catering for Parliamentary palates is not easy. There are 630 M.P.s in a full House. Their tastes vary violently and not always predictably.

Regularly, there are luncheon and dinner parties, large and small, in the dining rooms overlooking the Terrace and the Thames. The guests may take Graves or claret or Champagne or hock. But one day, an M.P. entertaining a group of Hungarians will want half-a-crate of Bull's Blood; or it may be Israelis or Australians or Californians or saki addicts who have to be wooed with their national beverage. Happily, many foreigners visiting the Commons opt for whisky, of which 3,124 bottles were sold last year.

In the old days, whisky had a splendid and awesome place in the conviviality of the Commons. Down in those cellars rested a vast vat, called the Valentia Vat after a Viscount

The Strangers' Bar

who was—unusually—both a Whip and popular. It held 1,000 gallons of Scotch, ten years' old, and was never drawn below a minimum of 400 gallons. There was also a smaller vat of Irish whiskey holding 300 gallons—and a selection of Royal sherries from Buckingham and St. James's Palaces and Windsor Castle.

Vintage Port used to be the popular potation—not unnaturally in what has been described as the finest club in London. But last year's sales perhaps reflect the nation's general change in taste—claret, 6,680 bottles; red burgundy, 4,680; Graves, 3,300; hock, 3,066; sherry, 2,800; white burgundy, 2,700; gin, 2,600; Champagne, 1,936; Moselle, 1,146; brandy, 863 and Port, a mere 640, of which 490 bottles were tawny at that! But, says Mr. Roberts: 'I am convinced vintage Port will become popular again'—and so he has laid down good stocks for drinking under the Space Age Government of 1984!

Typical of Westminster's curious blend of palace, club and legislative assembly is the freedom to drink within the Chamber itself (nothing to do with the phrase 'At the Bar of the Commons', which refers to the line on the floor at one end of the Chamber, marking its formal bounds).

In practice, only one M.P. today drinks in the House, and then but once a year—the Chancellor of the Exchequer, who customarily fortifies himself as well as the revenue during his Budget speech with what the newspapers used discreetly to describe as 'an amber-coloured liquid.'

There are rules to prevent M.P.s from

47

Two views of the Press Bar

taking swords into the Chamber (unless they are court officials). Other weapons, sticks or umbrellas (unless they need them to walk on), food to eat, or despatch cases (unless they are Ministers) are similarly forbidden. Until recently, there was doubt whether a carafe of water was permitted, one such having once been used as a missile! But there are no rules to prevent an M.P. from taking a bottle of Champagne or a glass of ale into the Chamber, and there consuming it at any time while the House is sitting.

The place, indeed, was much more of a public eating house 300 years ago. Members openly ate bread and cheese at the trial of Charles I; the Journals tell how the eating of nuts was common; Cecil Rhodes had stout and sandwiches brought to him daily when he was under examination before the South Africa Committee; and even smoking was permitted in the Chamber until 1693.

Speaking for three-and-a-half hours on the first Reform Bill in 1831, in a temperature of 85 degrees Fahrenheit, Lord Brougham sustained himself with copious draughts of mulled claret.

Gladstone, introducing his great Budget of 1860 in a four-hour harangue, took frequent swigs from a bottle containing 'a mixture of egg and wine, which Mrs. Gladstone had prepared.'

And so to Sir Stafford Cripps's lemon barley water (but he cut, dramatically, the wine and spirit duties!) Mr. Heathcoat Amory's rum and milk and honey, Mr. Selwyn Lloyd's brandy and water, and Mr. Reginald Maudling's hip flask of whisky, a reminder of the beverage that sustained Winston Churchill when he was Chancellor on Budget Day.

The tale is told of a 19th century M.P. who, well-laced, was heading purposefully for the Chamber. A kindly colleague steered him away to a cab, and to his home a mile away, got him to bed, and then, it being a fine night, strolled back to the Commons.

He returned to a packed Chamber. There was his merry friend, up, back and ebulliently eloquent, making the speech of his life!

Mr. A. M. Mitchell manages the Refreshment Department

Time has been called many times, but it has also brought changes since this article was written. Annie's bar has happily been reopened; on April 3rd, 1969, a notable occasion attended not only by the Prime Minister and the Speaker of the Commons, but by Annie herself.

There is now a new Refreshment Department Manager, Mr. André Maurice Mitchell, and he has given me the latest consumption figures.

Champagne has nearly doubled in popularity— 3,420 bottles at the current annual rate—and this is because there are now more wedding and other similar receptions in the Commons.

Claret is still the most popular wine—5,948 bottles a year, with red Burgundy (4,988) continuing as the runner-up. Brandy and Port (880 and 628 bottles respectively, still cannot compete with whisky (2,948 bottles) and gin (1,924). Sherry maintains a respectable 2,156 bottles a year.

A final thought—consumption of wines and spirits in the Commons seems to vary inversely with the size of the Government's majority. Up in 1964–66, when the Government's margin was minimal; down since the March 1966 General Election gave them a large majority which made it easier to release M.P.'s from constant attendance at the Commons.

GROG

by Harry Barton

From 1st August 1970, the rum ration is abolished. Thereafter sailors may buy three 12oz cans of beer a day, and petty officers buy ½ gill of any popular spirit available commercially.

As soon as we heard that the Royal Navy's rum ration was to be abolished we asked our Historical and Mathematical Editors for an analysis. The result was a rather rum graph:

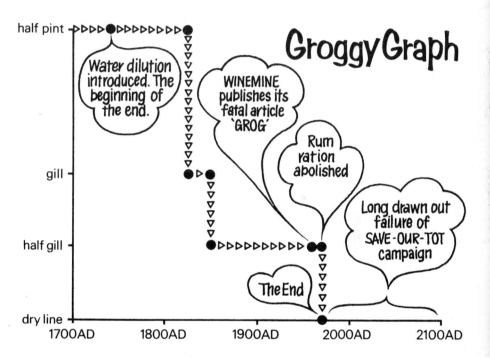

From this graph the discriminating drinker can note with sorrow how the ration grew smaller and smaller as the centuries passed. He will also notice that WINEMINE's 1962 article *Grog* has been followed, *within a decade,* by utter abolition.

Our inescapable conclusion is that the article caused the abolition. We are torn between pride in WINEMINE's power to affect naval policy and sorrow that we should have been the cause of the disappearance of the sailor's tot.

We reproduce the fatal article here. It was of course the disgusting idea of the little brown pellets that swayed the Admiralty Board. Better no ration at all, they must have decided, than swallow this Pill.

51

Admiral Vernon from the painting by Thomas Gainsborough

Until 1824 the daily ration of rum in the Royal Navy was half a pint. This is a terrible lot of rum; in alcoholic content, it represents twenty-eight modern small gins such as might be served in the wardroom of one of H.M. ships. The ration was issued in two whacks, one at dinner and one with the evening meal. Even the most rugged of expense-account tycoons, at the peak of his powers, riding high and racing ahead of the other rats, would pause before charging his firm for fourteen lunch-time gins per head of belly comfort—and then for another fourteen at dinner. But the British sailor has always been in a class by himself and look what happened to Napoleon.

Nevertheless, as early as 1740, the authorities had begun to feel that there was too much rum about. On the West Indies Station, Admiral Vernon sought to abolish the ration, making warm references to the 'swinish vice of drunkenness'; he failed in this, but did introduce the practice of diluting the raw spirit with water. He was already known as 'Old Grog', because of his habit of wearing a boatcloak made of a coarse fabric called grogram; and the new mixture was inevitably called 'grog', and has been so called ever since. Hence 'groggy' and 'grog-blossom'; but not, of course, 'merry as a grig' which only means among other things that you are as merry as a small eel.

In 1824, having brooded upon the watered half-pint for eighty-four years, Their Lordships of the Admiralty suddenly pounced; they reduced the ration by half, so that Jack now had only seven gins for dinner and seven for supper. Warming to their work, Their Lordships waited a mere twenty-six years before pouncing again, and again reducing the ration, this time down to the half gill a day that still obtains. The evening ration, in fact, disappeared. Simultaneously, they stopped the officers' issue and they introduced Grog Money; a sailor who elects not to take up his rum, is paid a money allowance instead. In 1850 this allowance was a penny a day and worth considering; today it is threepence and no one would notice the difference in his pay packet. Even a half gill is quite a deal of rum (one eighth of an imperial pint, or 2½ ounces),

especially as the Navy's rum is 90 proof, compared with the 70 proof of the ordinary whisky or gin. Chief petty officers and petty officers still receive their issue neat, but the others must have two parts of water added for every part of rum. Except in the Royal Canadian Navy. And before I tell you what the Royal Canadian Navy do, I wish to warn all inhabitants of Bournemouth and Cheltenham, together with all those who combine a high regard for tradition with a high blood pressure, to take a grip of themselves. The Royal Canadian Navy do not mix water into their rum; they mix in cola.

Today, the problem of the issue of rum afloat is a problem of time, space and motion study. Rum takes up space and its issue occupies much time for many people each day. This is because the whole affair is one of splendid and heart-warming tradition, and because it is essential to account for neat spirit very carefully and to the last tot. The modern warship is full of highly complicated devices, electronic and explosive, and is simply not suited to the wandering drunk, his smile beatific, his inspired fingers fumbling for buttons to press, wheels to turn and triggers to pull. At six bells of the forenoon watch, eleven o'clock, 'Up spirits' is piped. The Officer of the Day, in company with the Duty Petty Officer, the Duty Regulating Petty Officer, the Stores Petty Officer, and the Butcher (unfortunately there is not enough space in which to explain why it is that the ship's butcher must be in on this) proceed to the Spirit Room.

The Officer of the Day, to whose person its enormous key is attached, unlocks the armoured hatch and leads his men down vertical steel ladders into the spirit room, which, in a cruiser, will hold thirty or more kilderkins. From there he makes the issues of neat spirit to the chief petty officers' and petty officers' messes, each issue calculated precisely by the stores petty officer in relation to the numbers entitled on that day. The remainder of the day's issue is transferred from the large kilderkin to a small cask called a barrico, pronounced breaker, and this barrico is then padlocked and placed under the charge of a sentry until the issue is made to the remainder

Limbo dancers in Barbados, a prominent source of rum

of the ship's company at dinner-time.

Five minutes before dinner, the Rum Call is sounded on the bugle, and each mess sends its 'cook of the mess' to the rum tub with a jug or 'fanny'. At the big oaken rum tub, with its brass inscription, 'THE QUEEN GOD BLESS HER' a rigid ceremony is performed. The exact quantity of water is measured out and poured into the tub. The Officer of the Day then unlocks the barrico and the day's rum is tipped in with the water. The Officer of the Day, the Duty Regulating Petty Officer and the Stores Petty Officer stand round the tub, their eyes alert and wary. The first cook-of-the-mess steps forward. The Stores Petty Officers sings out the exact number of tots to which the particular mess is entitled on that particular day. The Butcher dips the appropriate brass measures into the tub and fills the cook's jug. When all issues have been made, the Butcher mournfully tips the residue into the scuppers, under the eye, still alert, of the Officer of the Day.

Officers only receive an issue of rum when the traditional order 'Splice the Main Brace' is given. In the days of sailing ships, the tough and dangerous task of splicing a new main yard-arm brace was often thought to merit an extra issue to all hands. Nowadays the signal 'Splice the Main Brace' is usually only made on royal occasions, upon the instructions of the Sovereign; or after a great victory, VE and VJ Days being examples of this last.

There is no doubt that the presence of rum in a modern warship wastes time and space, and in the modern warship there is little to spare of either. Equally, there is no doubt that it would be infinitely sad to lose this ancient ceremony and for the British sailor to lose his daily stomach-comfort. Perhaps the solution lies in dehydration. American scientists have finally managed to produce dehydrated water (what does it *look* like?) and it should not be beyond the ingenuity of Their Lordships to introduce tiny brown pellets of dehydrated rum. The ship's supply officer, after a short course in Hatton Garden on the art of keeping tabs on tiny objects of priceless value, could keep the lot in his money safe, issuing them daily, one at a time, to entitled customers. But this would be sad; also, 'THE QUEEN GOD BLESS HER' would look silly on a pill-box.

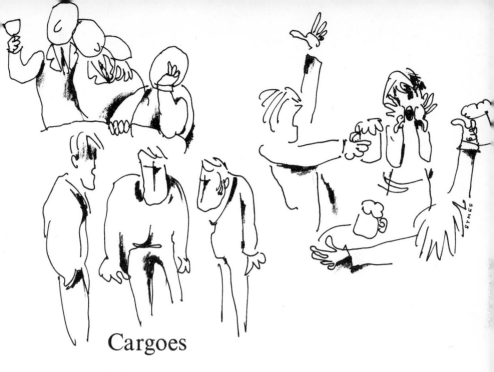

Cargoes

Gathering of brokers in a West End grillroom,
Sitting at the table until 4 p.m.,
*   With a cargo of Heidsieck*
*   And Schloss Johannisberg,*
Romanée Conti and Château Yquem.

Rowdy lot of youngsters in a Soho chophouse,
Honouring the birthday of a well-liked chum,
*   With a cargo of draught beer*
*   And gin and whisky,*
Pouilly, Beaujolais and Van der Hum.

Leather-coated teddies in an airless jazz-club,
Ready for a punch-up at the first excuse,
*   With a cargo of Pepsi,*
*   Tizer, Seven-up,*
Cappucino coffee and grape-fruit juice.

B. A. YOUNG

55

Prelate and Pirate. Midshipmen F. R. Twiss and J. F. B. Brown played Kayanne and Chili, Wards of The Bishop of Lee (Robert Burnett).

Wine, Ships and Song

by Anthony Hogg

In the naval world afloat between the wars, with women entirely absent and piped music still another (more welcome) absentee, it is hardly surprising that wine and music should have occupied many of 'our scanty hours of leisure.'

> *Ah in my scanty hours of leisure,*
> *Losing balls twixt tee and green,*
> *I might have spent my time ensuring*
> *That my intention was foreseen.*

The opera was by Gasolini, not exactly an original composer for the tune of this great Admiral's aria was none other than Verdi's Home to our Mountains from *Il Trovatore*.

Usually both our wine and song habits were less cultural. In the Gunroom a midshipman was allowed a wine bill of 15/– a month. Spirits were forbidden for those under 20 and since we went to sea from Dartmouth at the age of 17, this meant three years to wait before we could buy the proverbial pink gin. Beer (2d a glass) counted as wine, though in some lucky ships the Captain turned a blind eye to the regulations and beer for midshipmen became a teetotal drink, like Port to a Lancastrian. But it was surprising how far 15/– went. Sherry was 5d a glass, Port perhaps 6d. On Gunroom guest nights, the 'young gentlemen' contrived to live up to their name with three decanters—Port, Madeira and Marsala—being passed before the loyal toast. After dinner, at which the main dish was invariably Roast Blackcock, frozen as hard as an iron deck and similar in flavour, one could thaw out with Half a Corona for 10d!

The standard of 'song' was as high as could be expected from a Gunroom piano never tuned, though frequently lubricated with glasses of beer. But in the Wardroom—home of those with two and three stripes—musical entertainment was of a higher standard. After all, they were civilised; they had £5 wine bills!

In my half-dozen sea appointments during the '30s, there was hardly one without a ship's concert party. And if duty free liquor played a small part in their inspiration and execution, it undoubtedly played the lead as an inducement to the rest of the Fleet to fill the house.

My theatrical debut was in H.M.S. 'Rodney', which I had joined from Dartmouth with six other cadets. Within a few weeks of our arrival we were invited to the Wardroom for a voice trial. The result in due course was 'The Folies Bargee' chorus, playing the part of District Visitors in a 'Musical Extravaganza' called *Prelate and Pirate*.

> *'District Visitors always are ladies, are ladies,*
> *Of our smile every sinner afraid is, afraid is,*
> *But to the meritorious we,*
> *Dispense the savoury bread of charity.'*

Let no one claim that such brilliant verse was inspired by cocoa during the middle watch! Our librettist, the Engineer Commander, had a cabin alongside the Wardroom bar.

The prelude to the one performance was a week of showing the flag at Algiers, followed by a week of combined Mediterranean and Atlantic Fleet exercises, during which play and work respectively put a stop to all rehearsals.

Prelate and Pirate. The Verrey-Würst Male Choir rehearse The Pirates Chorus.
Left to Right: G. E. Creasey (Admiral of the Fleet), G. C. Dickens (Captain), F. J. C. Halahan (Captain), R. D. Watson (Vice-Admiral), G. K. Collett (Rear-Admiral), C. B. Tidd (Captain), T. C. Robinson (Commander), J. J. Casement (Captain), O. F. M. Wethered (Commander), G. N. Oliver (Admiral), H. T. Rust (Commander, killed in action 31.12.42), G. M. Wheadon (Lt.-Commander, invalided)
(The bracketed print following each name shows rank subsequently attained.)

Eventually, when both Fleets anchored off Palma Majorca, the stage was rigged on Rodney's quarter-deck in a day and the curtain went up in half a gale. My journal records the evening 'a great success', as well it might be! The starboard side of Rodney's immense forecastle had been rigged as a 'petrol' station where the guests helped themselves to gin and whisky from the pumps. Rodney's boats plied far into the small hours, taking officers back to the smaller ships in weather too rough for their own boats, while the shipwrights dismantled bars and stage. At 0900 the following morning when the Fleets sailed, there was no outward sign of our revels. Inwardly, as far as eight 'District Visitors' unaccustomed to drinking spirits were concerned, there was every sign.

The extra work caused by the officers' theatricals was not always popular with the ship's company. Stephen King-Hall and Ian Hay delighted London audiences with the opening scene of *The Midshipmaid* where a sailor was washing paintwork prior to some show.

'And the ship's company?' said a Cabinet Minister being shown round the ship by the Commander, 'I suppose they play a part in all this.'

'Oh, of course, Sir! They enter fully into the spirit of the thing.'

The sailor, played by A. W. Bascombe, turned towards the audience. He did not speak, the expression on his face was enough to bring the house down.

The reputation for the hardest drinking belonged to the destroyer flotillas. There was one ship where it was said that when the First Lieutenant and 'The Chief' sat down on the fender after lunch and ordered their first glass of port, you could put your watch right. It was always 4 p.m. precisely! But whatever went on in harbour, there was no drinking at sea. This was an unwritten small ship rule, only broken I remember, by one Captain commanding a flotilla, whose coxswain would bring him a large whisky and soda on the bridge at sunset. He was an Hon., which perhaps entitled him to be a rebel.

In H.M.S. Vidette, where I spent three months training, our drinking was enough to

Above: Austin 7 in Barbados 1932. R. L. W. Moss, E. T. Larken (at the wheel), J. A. V. Morse and A. S. Hogg.

Left: Prelate and Pirate. District Visitors Midshipmen M. F. Andrew, A. S. Hogg, F. P. Baker, R. E. Topp.

inspire enthusiasm for the concert party but not too great to become a major recreation. Later, the Captain and producer, Angus Nicholl, was to achieve fame in command of H.M.S. Penelope when she escaped from Malta—a story in which his own enthusiasm for 'song' did much to maintain a gallant ship's company's morale.

In January 1932, most of the 'District Visitors' joined the battle cruiser Repulse, sailing with the Hood and a squadron of cruisers for a cruise to the West Indies. For a week to the Azores there were continuous gales and a fair measure of Biscay water leaked into the Gunroom, aft and just above the water line. The usual Midshipmen's instruction was impossible. We waded about in sea boots, playing bridge and exhausting our wine bills too soon. But after the Azores the usual life of instruction, watchkeeping, fleet exercises, dog watch deck hockey and (of course) concert-party planning returned.

A Sail for a Sale was performed in the leading theatres of Port of Spain Trinidad, Grenada, St. Vincent and Barbados by an all-Repulse cast, sober yet saturated with rum cocktails. There were rum cocktails at Government House, at Tennis parties, on board after Church on Sundays and ashore after Rugby, played on bone-breaking grounds. The midshipmen who took part in these affairs, returning at 7 p.m. to take charge of a launch or a picket boat, can be thankful there was no breathalyser for boat runners.

The sensation of the show was a number called 'Operatic Motoring' where a car—an Austin 7—made its first appearance on the stage in the West Indies. Anthony Morse, the Commander of Repulse selected me (for what reason I never discovered except that he was particularly kind to midshipmen) to be his partner in a duet. As garage proprietor and mechanic, we sang topical verses to the tune of Offenbach's Gendarmes. What they were or why we were received in Barbados like Callas at Covent Garden, I cannot remember. But I suppose this is not surprising when you think of all those rum cocktails.

Called to the BAR

by Julian Jeffs

The two kinds of bars have much more in common than the name; for lawyers have always been fond of their wine. Dickens knew all about us. He was fully at home in the law courts, as he was in all the lesser inns and alleyways which in his day surrounded the four great Inns of Court. And in the wisdom of *Bleak House* he made the whole of Chancery symbolically and spontaneously combust. It was alcohol that brought this miracle to pass; and if spirits could really provoke such a doom, we should certainly have lost at least one Lord Chancellor long before he attained the woolsack.

Yes, if the law's delays occasionally drive a layman to drink, the lawyers themselves need no driving: they take to it naturally. It was so in the days of Mr. Serjeant Buzfuz, and it is so today. But, for the most part, they take to drink with discernment and not to excess. There is fine wine to be had around the Temple, and many a member of the Bar can boast a noble private cellar. The great tradition of good drinking is reflected in the famous silver owned by the Inns of Court and by the various circuits. If the humblest student of Gray's Inn orders nothing more than a pint of beer with his lunch, he will drink it out of a fine silver tankard. When he eats his dinners, he will be offered the choice of red or white table wines—decent *ordinaires* from Bordeaux. After he is called to the bar, he will drink sherry or port, as well—and usually both. At Grand Nights, when the

benchers entertain Very Important Persons, the ceremonials attain new heights. Each guest is gloriously announced with the utmost pomp. There is a loving cup. And there is a lot of champagne.

At dinner, the hall is presided over by Mr. Senior—the most senior member of the bar present. At the other end of the scale—and at the other end of the hall—is Mr. Junior, a post which falls to the lot of whichever student sits in the most junior position. This post is not sought after. Members of hall sit in messes of four, and during dinner each member must toast the other three. Then the mess as a whole toasts the messes above and below it. After grace has been said and the benchers have filed out to take their dessert and old vintage port in the decent seclusion of their private common-room, it falls to the lot of Mr. Junior to ask Mr. Senior for permission to smoke. And it often pleases his friends to make so much noise that Mr. Senior cannot hear. Sometimes, too, Mr. Senior is pleased not to hear. After order has eventually been restored, and the permission has been given—but not before—members may leave. Those remaining settle down for as long as they please with the coffee, and members of the bar messes have their port. More port may be ordered, and it often is. Then, too, the fun begins. If any member of hall has committed an offence—if he has proposed a toast incorrectly, or if he has sat at table in the wrong order of seniority, or if he is wearing a 'white coat', to name the three most popular charges—he is accused by another member of hall, and he is expected to defend himself. The case is heard by Mr. Senior, and if the member is found guilty he is fined a 'a bottle of port', which in practice is commuted to four glasses, that cost him five shillings. Of all these offences, the most common is the 'white coat'. Black coats are obligatory, and they have to be jet black. Any colour that is not black is white, and a black coat with a white stripe is regarded as a white coat with a black stripe. The rest of one's attire has to be respectable, too. When I was a student, long years ago, I construed the rule too narrowly and arrived wearing a black coat over a pair of jeans. I was fined two bottles of port—one for each leg.

The benchers have already been referred to. To give them their full title, they are Masters of the Bench—the self-appointed governing body which rules each inn. It is they who have the power to call a student to the bar and to suspend a barrister from practice or to disbar him for misconduct, though they have recently delegated the latter powers to the Senate of the four Inns of Court. Like the dons at a university, they dine apart from the rest of hall, at the high table; and the sight of their food, with the legend of their cellar, is enough to spur any young barrister on in his profession.

For the purpose of assizes and quarter sessions, the country is divided up into a number of circuits, each of which has its own customs, traditions and, of course, cellars. And the glory of their cellars is invariably the vintage port. Each term the circuit entertains the assize judge to dinner. On the Oxford Circuit this is usually done in Gloucester on commission day. Sometimes other great figures of the law are entertained: the Lord Chancellor, for instance, or the Lord Chief Justice. At these dinners fine wines are served in worthy quantities. Old bottled sherry to begin; hock or moselle with the fish; champagne with the main course, or claret, as an alternative; then the old vintage port comes out.

Grand nights are less formal and more delightful meetings of the circuit. They are held in assize towns and the Oxford Circuit holds one a year in an Oxford college. The wines, on these occasions, are less exotic, but there are other attractions. After dinner, the 'Attorney-General', or 'Solicitor-General' of the circuit prefers indictments against any member guilty of a 'crime'. If, for example, he has been appointed a recorder, or has taken silk, he has certainly obtained the post by the false pretence that he has sufficient knowledge of the law; if his photograph has been in the paper, he has been guilty of indecent exposure; if he has

RODNEY SYMES

63

dared to marry, who knows what crime he might not have committed? But he always has the right to be represented. It is the custom for his counsel to say a few felicitous words in aggravation rather than in mitigation, and the enormity of his crime is properly brought home to the criminal. The fines, of course, are exacted in wine: a case of port from an old lag, half a case for a younger man or for a more trivial crime, and a very young man whose only crime has been his marriage may actually be granted a conditional discharge. The fines help to swell the cellar, and apart from these, until recently when a barrister went 'special' on a circuit other than his own he was expected to give a present of wine or of silver. When this article first appeared in WINEMINE, it cost its author *two* cases of port.

Prosecuting, on these occasions, is an art; and the best-loved 'Attorney-General' of the Oxford Circuit within recent memory was Stephen Benson. Recorder of Abingdon for many years, his sheer humanity made him one of the best recorders in the country. And, as an advocate, he was one of the few who really could laugh a case out of court. On one occasion, when he was sitting as recorder, he took a very humane chance and put an old lag on probation. After telling him what this meant, and warning him with due severity about the future, he finished with the words: 'And I hope I may never see you again'. He relaxed and sat back in his chair. Then he added, as an afterthought: 'Of course, I don't mean socially'.

Only a good wine drinker could have known humanity as he did. And while the bar remains close to the cellar, there will not be much amiss with the law.

M. A. Deira by Robert Gittin

When I first went to Cambridge Coll.
A Doctor of Divinity
Gave words of wis. that spoke a vol.
To those in his vicinity.
He cried: 'From all the history
Of our great Christian era,
Note down one-four-two-owe A.D.—
Discovery of Madeira!

Four centuries supremely good
This wine ruled England's salons;
In eighteen-twenty, imports stood
At half a million gallons.
O what a falling-off was there!
O tempora, o mores!
So you, young man, must now repair
Its fame, and sing its glories.

Who can describe it? Who can catch
Its flavour, brisk, volcanic?
Milton's great poem could not match
This Angel half-satanic.
From Sercial keen to Malmsey bland
It runs the palate's gamut.
Youngman, youdrinkit! Understand!—
Or you'll be sent down, dammit!'

Come, praise this wine by night and day
To all your generation
Till once again our land is a
Madeira-drinking nation.
And if they snidely ask you why
Your Muse such claims advances,
Come to the fount of learning: I
Will tell you all the answers!

So spoke the sage. I meekly conned
The subject of his lecture,
Tried it, and found it true, beyond
All possible conjecture:
And now that Learning's door is shut,
And Age is growing nearer,
These letters to my name I put—
'B.A. and M.A.(deira)'.

Before and after dinner, you
May drink it with impunity,
Aperitif, dessert-wine too,
Both in one blessed unity.
As for that modern horror, which
(I hear) is called elevenses,
This liquor, golden, dry, yet rich
Puts one in seventh heavens.

Alfred Perry, now retired but still enjoying golf, sent his photograph at my request. In the thirties, I had the pleasure of knowing him on the Leatherhead course and at the nineteenth, presided over by the Steward, Ex-Sick Berth C.P.O. Alright, a character who helped to save my life by administering less pleasant fluids at a naval hospital when I was wounded in 1940.

—Editor

Alfred Perry ('superb control of glass and club alike') Open Champion at Muirfield 1935.

The Nineteenth Hole

by L. G. Crawley

I hope we golfers can exercise as much restraint as the next man, consistent of course with providing the alcoholic custom my readers will look for. Still, the fact remains that, to the 18 holes traditionally associated with a round of golf, there is added a 19th, where we are wont to chew over our successes and failures, and it is unthinkable that we should do so in barley-water.

In various other lands refreshment is more immediately available. In the United States—where they are generally a jump ahead of us in these matters—it is possible for the small outlay of 200 dollars—and many people would be prepared to pay that in order to slake the thirst they acquire on the golf-course—to hire a helicopter which, like some St. Bernard of the skies, is equipped with a life-giving fluid and which will come to the rescue on request. While in one of our Crown Colonies—when we still had such things—I remember reading of a course which dodged its way among the bungalows, and where, by the simple expedient of taking too powerful a weapon for the tee-shot at the 11th, it was possible to end up on a verandah where drinks were dispensed by a boy at all times when golf was in season.

In these islands it is seldom customary to drink anything 'hard' while the actual game is in progress—perhaps because we play it more expeditiously than they do across the Atlantic. But our thoughts towards the end of a round tend to concentrate more and more upon the drink with which we will eventually crown it. And few of us like to set out on one entirely 'dry'. The late James Braid spoke for many of us, when he said that he always liked to be 'a wee bit nervous' before an important en-

Henry Cotton, Open Champion, Muirfield 1938

counter. Golf *is* a nerve-engendering pastime—especially on the green. And there is no surer way of acquiring that confidence which golf demands than by lowering at least one drink before we set off. Surely Bertie's criterion of the well-equipped golf-course would be, as it was of so many country-houses, that 'both the browsing and sluicing were above reproach'.

The only question that exercises one—and would possibly even have exercised Bertie Wooster—is what drink is most suitable for the purpose. We need one to instil courage—whether Dutch or the real variety—without impairing judgement. And such a drink—if I may respectfully suggest as much to gentlemen whose occupation is the provision of liquor—has yet to be invented.

A friend of mine recommends the Cherry Whisky which used to be served in that tin shack which once did duty as Rye Golf Club, and is now the most comfortable Club house on an English golf links, because it made the ball look enormous, and—for him at any rate—the difficulty in striking it normally lay in its diminutive size. But even if he is right, his lore is purely academic now, because a 'doodle-bug' during the War destroyed the Rye Club House together with its total contents. And though my friend has instituted a pious pilgrimage over most of the world, his search has so far proved unavailing.

Kummel is said to be a very good putting-mixture; and perhaps the Royal Calcutta Golf Club possesses the true elixir. They add a dash of whisky to it, and call it Whummel. If a class-player arises from the banks of the Hooghly, we shall know they were right.

Bobby Jones was less successful than my friend in his experiences with sherry. He drank a glass at St. Andrews before his afternoon match against George Voigt, and only just recovered his powers of judging distance in the nick of time. As he went on to win the 'Impregnable Quadrilateral'—this was in 1930—we cannot hold the produce of Jerez entirely guiltless on this occasion. On others he was less abstemious, and only quitted drinking when he quitted golf.

The late Walter Hagen also 'went on the waggon' at the end of his illustrious career as a golfer—I suppose with some vague idea of prolonging his terrestial existence. In this he was abundantly successful. But at a price! His putting—once so notable—forsook him immediately he renounced alcohol, and he never won another competition. Far otherwise was the case of George Duncan, who played fine (alcohol-inspired) golf up to the time of his death.

I must mention Cotton as a 'dry' player. His fourth round in the Open of 1934 was typical of such cold-blooded methods—and accomplished, moreover, with stomach cramp. I have no reason whatever for adducing alcoholic stimulation, but Perry's last round of the year after was much more that of a man who has had a drink. As I say, I have no valid reason for stating that Perry had. I am merely saying that he played with that carefree abandon that suggests superb control of glass and club alike.

I played other games besides golf, and so perhaps I may be forgiven if I find myself straying into other paths. Cricket was my first love, and it is therefore natural to remember the men who played it best. A. C. Maclaren was born some thirty years before me, and I cannot claim to have seen him in action in his prime, yet his name comes down to me as an imperial—and sometimes imperious—batsman, who made his many runs on something other than tea. But Walter Hammond was roughly my contemporary—Hammond, who if he could avoid it, would never watch the batsmen before him in a Test. This idiosyncrasy was probably just nerves, of which the general public were never permitted to see any manifestation when the great man strode forth to do battle himself. But I submit that it can be partially accounted for by the fact that Hammond had something better to do with his pre-batting time. It is said that he had no less than seven pink gins before he made his 240 at Lord's.

All men are made differently, and it is from their infinite variety that the great figures—impartially—are drawn. Happily it is impossible to pontificate. But most men like a drink before the game to settle intrusive nerves, and another after it to drown their sorrows.

Walter Hammond ('seven pink gins before he made his 240').

The Sparklers

by Denzil Batchelor

It is, I think, June Forsyte who somewhere in the *Saga* refuses wine, saying that she hates the horrid, sour stuff. Sparkling burgundy might have been made for her—it is a wine made for people who don't like wine: a wine for people who like deb dances, garden fêtes, lawn tennis parties, lolling in punts on hot summer evenings; and a nice change (if you like) from Black Velvet. In other words it is, if not a red rag to a bull, at least a burgundy rag to a connoisseur, who is sure to tell you that the quintessence of burgundy, its rich depths, and the shallow sparkle of this thirst-quencher, are poles apart.

Don't forget, however, that the wine is much drunk in France where perhaps they have more hot summer evenings and garden fêtes—and certainly fewer wine snobs. I could not conscientiously recommend Sparkling burgundy (red) as a wine for connoisseurs, but perhaps I should mention (before you decide once and for all) that in the old days before World War I it was a particular favourite of ladies of easy virtue and also for young girls who were inclined to wish that their own virtue wasn't quite so difficult.

The fates are unkind to sparkling wines other than champagne, even those made by the costly Méthode Champenoise. As far as production costs and taxes are concerned these are treated on all fours with champagne itself. Well, if you are to be charged 18s 9d for sparkling red burgundy and 25s 3d for non-vintage Mercier, most people, realising the snob value of the champagne image and the anti-sparkling burgundy campaign among wine-experts in this country, will plump for the champagne without the least hesitation. You ask the next dozen wine-drinkers you meet what they think of Sparkling red burgundy; and you will get twelve rude answers. Then ask how many of them have actually ever drunk Sparkling red burgundy—and the answer, if truthful, will be *none*.

Once again, I am only suggesting the refreshing tipple for the June Forsytes of this world: for those who like a thirst-slaking, palate-tickling drink on a hot afternoon—not —emphatically not—for those who think burgundy is sacred and who mentally present arms when passing the vineyards of Vougeot. I don't have to recommend it to Americans: they already drink plenty of it from the rock-bound coast of Maine all the way westwards.

We drink, in this country, nearly two million gallons of sparkling wines a year, of which just over half is champagne.

EYE OF THE PARTRIDGE

Among the more interesting of the French imports are sparkling white burgundy and Oeil de Perdrix—Partridge Eye—a Sparkling pink burgundy recently introduced into this country after achieving a formidable success in agricultural districts on its home front. I have drunk with pleasure both these beverages. Sparkling white burgundy is not, and doesn't pretend to be champagne. The best of it is made

Fontanafredda's sparkling Asti is the centre of this trio of Piedmont wines taken against the background of the former Royal hunting lodge, which is part of their Establishment, near Alba.

by the Méthode Champenoise, but the wine has, if less elegance, a greater fruitiness, and is good enough to last well—I recently drank a 10 year old sparkling white burgundy and found the colour deepened, the bead still large and lasting: and the wine itself a refreshing thirst-quencher from the commune of Rully on the Côte Chalonnaise made mainly from the champagne grape, the Pinot Blanc.

Cristal Dry, I have no doubt is popular with parents of brides with unwieldy wedding parties on their hands but I think that more and more brides (rather than battleships) may be launched with the Partridge Eye. It's a pink sparkling burgundy: and when it was itself launched a few years ago at a party at the Victoria, Lancaster Gate (where the furnishings include part of the dress-circle of the old Gaiety Theatre) its unpretentious charm and unsophisticated elegance won, I think, a unanimous vote of confidence. It wasn't just a hot day thirst-quencher for girls: it was good enough for a hirsute golfer coming in after 36 holes in a heat wave. This drink was worth keeping in the 'fridge as long as any rumour of summer lingers in the weather forecasts. No sugariness—no feeling that you are drinking a lollipop melted from its stick.

Among the lesser sparklers is one from Vouvray on the Loire which in pre-war days gave us Veuve Amiot, one of the most popular wines of its modest class. Those who have won top prizes at shooting galleries at French fairs know its fresh demi-sec flavour, unless of course they chose the outsize teddy bear that is the alternative prize to a bottle of Méthode Champenoise.

Sparkling Muscatel Golden Guinea is for wine-drinkers with a very sweet tooth, since it is made from the succulent Muscat grape. I think it is for girls rather than for men—and not for all girls at that.

STRAUSS NOT MOZART

The Germans make their wine sparkle in three ways: the Méthode Champenoise; the tank method, in which side-stepping the costly processes of *remuage* and *dégorgement,* the secondary fermentation is carried out in a closed enamelled steel tank—which, according to L. W. Marrison, produces a wine whose sparkle is of Strauss rather than Mozart; and finally—for home consumption only—the Impregnation Method, in which carbonic-acid gas is pumped into a high alcohol wine.

They have been making sparkling wines in Germany since 1826, from the grapes used to make champagne. German wine-sellers are not so foolish as to challenge a comparison with champagne, but their most attractive sparkling hocks and moselles are attractive to drink in warm weather. The Fürst Blücher Deutscher Sekt Mosel is good value indeed—fresh, light, adequately dry, a true symbol of gaiety in spite of the inhibiting picture of Blücher on the label If you measured it against poets and playwrights, I should call it a witty Sir John Suckling or perhaps a lively Congreve: not a Keats nor a Sheridan.

The sparkling Deinhard Cabinet and Liebfraumilch Blue Nun are much lighter in hand—one had almost said more frolic—than the still Hocks of these renowned names. But the Blücher, like the best of Sparkling moselles, is jocund indeed: no wonder more than ten million bottles of this type of wine is drunk every year.

Yes, the minor sparkling wines have their supporters—and why not? They are not champagne. They are not so to speak, Shakespeare—but because Shakespeare existed, I would not have Herrick and Prior, Swinburne and Flecker extirpated. The best must never be allowed to be the enemy of what so much innocent youth and beauty finds good for its purpose.

Whether it was some obscure facet of sport or of wine, Denzil could always interest and amuse either in an article or 'replying for the guests' at some function. His death in 1969 left a gap in The Circle of Wine Writers impossible to fill.
—Editor.

Georgian Wine Glasses

by William Gill

When William Gill was asked why a qualified architect, town planner and barrister, such as himself, should be an authority on Georgian wine glasses, he replied that his family had always needed wine glasses having been in the Law for over five hundred years.

The classical age of English wine glasses began in the year 1676, when George Ravenscroft of London discovered a new medium for glassmaking, that of lead-flint crystal. During the next hundred and fifty years, even though, due to war, French wines were almost ousted in Britain by those of Spain and Portugal, English glass became supreme in Europe. English wine glasses are classified by the shape of their stems and not of their bowls, and there are seven periods, or epochs, from 1680 to about 1830 which are as follows:

1 The Baluster Stem Period 1680 to 1725
2 The Light Baluster Stem Period 1715 to 1745
3 The German or Moulded Pedestal Period 1715 to 1750
4 The Plain Straight Stem Period 1720 to 1770 and later
5 The Air Twist Stem Period 1730 to 1770
6 The Enamel Twist Stem Period 1745 to 1780
7 The Facet or Cut Stem Period 1750 to 1800 and later

There are, of course, offshoots of these main groups, such as the incised twist stem glasses, hollow stem glasses, and others. The periods also overlapped, and after 1770 all glasses became smaller owing to the crippling taxes on lead-flint and on enamel imposed by the Glass Excise Acts of 1746, 1777 and 1787. From 1770, there appeared many types of glasses not enumerated above, such as Runmers or Grog glasses, dwarf Ale glasses, drams and jelly glasses, all of which persisted until the early Victorian era.

Apart from glasses for ale and champagne, English wine glasses were used for all types of wine. Ale was a strong barley wine of enormous alcoholic strength, and must be distinguished from beer, the drink of the working population. Champagne became popular because of the taste of King George II; the earliest champagne glasses were tazza-shaped, changing to the long flute bowl about 1730, and returning to the tazza or cup shape after 1830. The ale glass would have hop leaves and barley stalks engraved on the bowl after 1740; other glasses would have appropriate engravings, the vine tree or grapes for wine glasses, apples for cyder glasses, and so on. One of the illustrations shows a series of rare champagne, or sweetmeat glasses, dating from about 1700 to 1750. They include baluster, moulded pedestal, Newcastle light baluster, air-twist and hollow stems.

I will now deal briefly with the types of glasses:

BALUSTER STEM GLASSES

Heavily built and finely made of dark lead metal. The stems were of inverted balusters and true balusters with or without balls or knops on the stem. The bowls were at first conical and straight sided, later they became waisted like a bell shape, the feet were large, and folded at the edges, and sometimes domed and folded. There were certain rare special types of stem, such as a hollow cylinder which is shown by the first glass in the photograph, purchased by the author's ancestor, in London

'Opaque Enamel 1765'   'Facet 1760'   'Rummer 1775'

in 1710. Baluster glasses were rarely decorated except for 'blows', which are tears of air imprisoned in the base of the bowl or in the stem. Prices vary but most baluster glasses run into hundreds of pounds and are much prized.

LIGHT BALUSTER GLASSES
These were of the same style as baluster glasses but of lighter metal and shape. At first, as in the specimen shown in the illustration, they were almost identical with the heavy balusters but from about 1730 they became much smaller and lighter. The glass illustrated is a fine specimen of about 1720, with a large knop in the stem, a trumpet-shaped bowl, and a folded foot. The light baluster glasses were also undecorated, and relied on the quality of the glass. The glass illustrated is known as a

'Kit-Cat' glass. Very fine specimens were made in Newcastle-on-Tyne of almost silvery metal and are now very expensive to buy.

MOULDED PEDESTAL GLASSES
These were introduced from Germany by the Hanoverian kings, and as wine glasses their vogue was but twenty years, although they continued to be used as sweetmeat glasses until 1760. They are very fine glasses with stems moulded of four, and six-sided pedestals, later eight-sided pedestals, The photograph is of a wine glass of 1715. It has an engraved round funnel bowl, and a folded foot. These glasses died out without influencing the main stream of English glass design. As wine glasses they are now very rare and collectors offer large sums for them.

'Facet 1790'   'Port 1800'

before cooling it off. Modern glasses which are machine made, do not possess pontil marks, but there are fakes which deliberately copy the antique glasses, and the reader is warned against them. Plain-stem glasses are now becoming scarce, a good specimen could cost £15 or more.

AIR TWIST GLASSES

The imprisoned bubbles of air in the stem of the preceding glasses were sometimes joined together and this gave birth to the air twist stem. Spirals of air were formed in the stem, at first in a simple manner, but by 1750 in a beautiful design. At first the glassmen could only make a multiple spiral twist, which is shown in the rare and early glass in the photograph. The stem is shaped like an inverted baluster. Later, there were cables of spiral gauze, corkscrews of mercury and spiral threads and columns. Many of these glasses have trumpet bowls and plain feet, although folded feet occur in one glass in five. These typically English glasses are great favourites with collectors but some of them are very rare indeed.

OPAQUE ENAMEL TWIST GLASSES

After the Act of 1745 the glassmen were forced to make smaller glasses which contained less lead-flint, and had to depend on ornament to attract attention. Thus, the Continental white enamel twist became fashionable, and replaced the air twist stem by 1760. Rods of white or coloured enamel were drawn through the stem and allowed to cool with the outer skin. In 1777, a tax was placed on enamel and these glasses died out immediately. There are three types of twist, the single, double and triple twist. Eight glasses out of ten are of double series twist, whilst at the other end of the scale, a triple twist stem would be one glass in a thousand. The exquisite glass illustrated is an ale glass of 1765, 8 inches high, with an engraved bowl of hop leaves and barley, a triple twist stem and a high plain foot. The varieties of twists are endless in these glasses, and consist of spirals, tapes, threads and corkscrews of all sorts and sizes. Like air twist glasses, they are also becoming scarce and good specimens cost at least £30.

PLAIN STRAIGHT STEM GLASSES

These were made in their thousands from 1720 onwards, and were the glasses of the People. They have every type of bowl, bell, waisted, wind funnel, ogee, bucket, trumpet and ovoid. In the early period, before 1735, their stems, or bowl bases, sometimes contained a 'blow' or tear of air, as shown in the specimen illustrated, which dates from the Baluster period, and has a heavy waisted bowl and large folded foot. After 1745 the feet would be plain and high at the centre. Later in the century, the feet became smaller and flatter, and glasses in the 19th century had their feet of smaller diameter than of the bowl. All these antique glasses have a rough mark under the foot where the stem is joined to it, called a pontil or 'punty' mark where the glassman broke off the molten glass

'Baluster 1700'   'Moulded Pedestal 1740'   'Newcastle Light Baluster 17

'Baluster 1710'   'Light Baluster 1715'   'Moulded Pedestal 1715

'Twist 1750' 'Hollow Stem 1750'

'n Straight 1720' 'Air-Twist 1735'

FACET OR CUT STEM GLASSES

These became fashionable after 1760, and with the disappearance of the White twist glasses in 1780, they were supreme until the early 19th Century. The cut stems were fashioned in the shapes of diamonds, hexagons and vertical flutes. Where the bowl is cut as well, the higher the cutting on the bowl the later the glass. There are two facet-cut glasses illustrated, a wine glass of 1760, and a sherry glass of 1790. The former has a cut ogee bowl, diamond cut facet stem and a plain foot, whilst the latter has a plain vertical fluted stem and a funnel bowl.

LATER GEORGIAN AND REGENCY GLASSES

From 1770 onwards to 1830, most glasses were much smaller and lighter, almost all had short stems and smaller, plain feet. From 1770 to 1830, rummer or grog glasses were popular, generally with fluted ovoid bowls, as shown in the photograph. This rummer was purchased by an ancestor of mine on 8 July 1775. Some rummers were of enormous size, and some had square pedestal feet after 1790. There were also port wine glasses, as in the specimen dated 1800, shown in the illustration. There were drams with thick feet for thumping the table, known as firing glasses. The variety of bowls was endless, and engraved glasses became frequent. Some depicted hunting scenes and, after 1830, even railway engines. Whilst many of these later glasses are very pretty, and vastly superior in design to modern glasses, they are generally of a much poorer metal than the glasses of the Jacobean, early and middle Georgian eras, and of course much cheaper to buy. The reader becoming interested in old glasses should begin very carefully by choosing one specimen of each period at a time; a visit to the local museum, or gallery, to study these beautiful relics beforehand is essential for the student or the amateur collector.

BOTH HOBBY AND INVESTMENT

The hobby of antique glass collecting has grown enormously in recent years. Most glasses are twenty times the price when I first began collecting over thirty years ago. What will happen in the next thirty years requires more than a mere collector to prophesy.

79

WineMine Competitions

A Literary Competition (inspired by The *New Statesman*) has appeared in nearly every Winter number since 1960. The first, at a time when the duty on port had just been reduced, invited replies to the 'outrageous anti-port propaganda' contained in the eighteenth century verse:

Firm and erect the Caledonian stood.
Sweet was his mutton and his Claret good.
'Thou shalt drink Port' the English statesman cried;
He drank the poison and his spirit died.

1st Prize—£10 in wine
Mr J. P. Ricks of Barnet. Herts.

Poison, you say! The Scot was soon to find
That Port would nerve the sinews, soothe the mind.
Balance the humours, till by Port redeemed
Mutton ambrosia, claret nectar seemed.
Years passed; harsh Duty snatched again the bowl
Where Pleasure lay for every Scottish soul;
Till Amory, crying; 'Down with Duty!' brought
To Scots once more their Pleasure and their Port.

2nd Prize—£5 in wine.
Mr B. Burton of Stockport.

The Caledonian's spirit soon revived
When the wise scheme Methuen had contrived
Brought gold from Portugal to buy his wool
And coffers bulged from Berwickshire to Mull.
Converted from his wild untutored ways
He learned to give to Port its proper praise.
And drank to Heathcoat Amory, when he took
A leaf (God bless him!) from Methuen's book.

3rd Prize—£3 in wine.
Mr J. Finnie of Balham, London.

Beneath the sun-warmed Haggis trees
The placid Scots now take their ease.
While, cabers sheathed, they mildly laze
And watch their brave, black sporrans graze.
No longer feuds, nor fiery cross
Nor curses at the English Boss.
So runs the change in Scottish Mores
Since Port displaced the Doch an Dor's.

One bottle of Port.
Mr P. Cranmer of Belfast.

O you hard hearts, you cruel men of Margaux,
Wherefore on Port place you this fell embargo?
Knew you not Cockburn? Many a time and oft
You must have dined with Sandeman or Croft.
Are you not mindful of your marriage vow:
'With all my worldly goods I thee en-Dow?'
Go go, good countrymen, and with this thought:
The proper study of mankind is Port.

1961—ABOMINIC ATOMINIC DOMINIC: When the United States Atomic Energy Commission named a series of nuclear tests in the atmosphere *Operation Dominic,* the chance was too good to miss. 'Why', we asked, 'should a wine merchant, who had never launched anything more explosive than a large bottle, be singled out for this association without so much as a by your leave. B. A. Young, then Deputy Editor of Punch and now theatre critic for the Financial Times, reported:

No fewer than two hundred and eight-five poet-oenophiles had a go at this, a fair number of them more than once. They encompassed every kind of variation permissible within, or not within, the rules; there were a couple of double acrostics; there were parodies of Omar Khayyám and Gray's Elegy; there was a coloured drawing of a worried man treading grapes. Stern devotion to duty confined judgement to the strict observation of the terms of reference; otherwise I would have been tempted toward a complimentary bottle to Manchester's D. Burns for the handwriting alone.

'Dominic' seems to have proved a difficult rhyme. No less than five competitors had to invent the word 'atominic'; let them take heart from Mrs W. J. Mahood of Bangor, whose entry I quote in full for the rhymes alone—

How dare the U.S.A.E.C. usurp the name of
    Dominic!
The action's starkest tragedy—decidedly
    Melpomenic.
Imagine the reactions of all those who'd ban
    the bomb (in 'nick'–
Or out); the name of your dear 'Gov' to them
    will have become iniq–
–uitous! The Pentagon's to blame. 'Twas
    there, some wretched hominy c–
–onsuming clerk, who gave the name—
    'Coke'-full—was suffering from an hic–
–cup. What he meant was 'Dominus'. Foul
    Harry, Dick, or Tom! Ine⟩ –
–⟨picable crime! To sully thus the gracious
name of Dominic!

The typographical fission of the letter 'x' in lines fourteen and fifteen may be a poetic weakness, but it seems to me rather appropriate in the context.

What I looked for was some play on ideas,

rather than straightforward well-what-name-could-be-better treatment that accounted for three-quarters of the entries. (I also looked for competitors who could count up to eight and did not submit verses of either six or sixteen lines.) I like James Finney's entry for the 'wine-glass cloud', though I'm not sure if he is 'go' for either congratulation or condolence—

While James outwits sly SMERSH's blondes,
And ERNIE deals with other bonds,
When hurricanes are FLO, with neuter
UNIVAC a mere computer;
But comes that wine-glass cloud, that slow
And spreading heat and lasting glow,
And then we hail this global kick
'All systems go for DOMINIC'.

The same reservation applies to Eric Yates ('a fairly young man recently introduced to the delights of the grape'), but this entry has the genuine bouquet of poetry about it—

DOMINIC DIRIGE NOS.
Fearful of 'fall-out' and 'flashes' on high
Atoms and awesome attacks from the sky:
What is the maximum strontium dose?
DOMINE DIRIGE NOS.

Comforting solace, deep-hidden in wine;
Rollicking parties, with drinks good and fine,

Banish the dread of our dreams lachrymose:
DOMINIC DIRIGE NOS.

More in the tradition of light verse is S. G.
Truscott, though I'd have liked to know more
about this articulate bird he quotes from—

Said the apoplectic parakeet, 'It really makes
 you sick!
The way we have been used by 'Operation
 Dominic',
To see our lovely South Sea Isles enveloped
 in a flash,
By radio-active fall-out and thermo-nuclear
ash!'

But for Dominic of Horsham, let us give a
 hearty cheer,
There's not a sign of fall-out in the stuff they
 pour out here.
Though, from lack of moderation, as your
 footsteps homeward hover,
You may find yourself assailed by alcoholic
 'topple-over'.

D. Shepherd also displays a neat talent for
versification, not to mention some sound
advice for The Day—

In the States they drink coke, or else bourbon
 or rye,
While they ponder the problem of how we
 shall die,
So it's purely by chance that the Atom
Commission
Should think of your name as a cover for
 fission,
It's annoying, of course, but remember, I
 pray,
The cellar's the place if a bomb comes your
 way.
And if Dominic-stocked, both the craven and
 brave
Can at least meet their fate on the crest of the
wave.

Similar advice, perhaps not quite so stylishly
parcelled up, comes from John Comben,
one of many competitors for whom the name
Dominic suggested Dominus—

The men of Science, seeking for a name
To give this move in the atomic game
(On which they say the Nation's future hangs)
Suggest *Dominus,* the Lord of Bangs.

'But,' said the President, 'the way we're
 bound
The Nation's future will be underground.
Well—living in a cellar could be fine—
So let's say *Dominic* and order wine.'

Lest I should be accused of keeping out all those
competitors who went in for the congratu-
latory, what I have called the what-name-
could-be-better, approach, here is a neat
version from Ian Nicholson—

Who steals my purse steals trash. You stole
My name, for this your latest piece of fission,
Is this commission of another Sin,
Or sin of the Commission?
'Let's not fall-out', the Yanks reply,
'For though without so much as 'By your
 leave',
We took your name; what stratospheric
 heights
Will Dominic now achieve?'

I have left till last two entries from the same
address in Kuala Lumpur, from Patricia
Ambler and Dennis Ambler. They jostle one
another closely for first prize, and indeed did so
before I noticed their common origin. I will
quote first from Mrs Ambler—

Old words like wine-bottles retain their
 shape;
Meanings like clarets change with age.
 Today
The once so warlike phrase 'a whiff of grape'
Merely suggests a mellowed wine's
 bouquet.

Years hence, when this *new* Dominic so
 alarming
 Has petered out, all radiation spent,
Still shall *old* Peter Dominic, disarming,
 'Radiate' his wines to make the heart
 content.

And finally, with my recommendation for first prize, on the strict understanding that Mrs Ambler has not been helping him with his homework, the entry of Mr Ambler—

The ancient Greeks, avenging Fates to please,
Named them unaptly the Eumenides
(The Kindly Ones), and when they made a black

Hoped thus to put these hell-hounds off their track.
Might not our cousins by the self-same token
Have chosen for their tests a name that's spoken
With warm respect even by that old Commy Nik*?
What *could* be wrong in something labelled Dominic?

i.e. Communist Nikita Khruschev

1963 THE TRAVELLER: Setter Anthony Hogg. Judge B A Young.

'Is there anybody there?, said the Traveller
Knocking on the moonlit door;

Most readers will be familiar with Walter de la Mare's poem 'The Listeners—'

For he suddenly smote on the door, even
Louder, and lifted his head—
'Tell them I came, and no one answered,
That I kept my word,' he said.
Never the least stir made the listeners . . .

I have often wondered what was the 'inside story' leading up to this intense moment of drama and anti-climax. What was the promise responsible for The Traveller's eerie errand and why was there no one but the phantom listeners to greet him?

Competitors were asked to give rein to their own views in not more than 8 lines of verse in the same metre as the original. The only condition imposed was that either The Traveller or the Missing Householder was a wine-merchant.

Report by B A Young—I read through all the entries, and they weren't very many; and then I went out and drank a stiff measure of Hennessy XO and came back and read them again, and this time they looked a little better. But there's no doubt, I fear, that the conditions we set for our poet-oenophiles proved a bit too daunting this time.

The first to be eliminated were the ones who ignored the conditions altogether and sent verse on a subject of their own choosing or to a metre of their own choosing. Even if they had offered us something as fine as Keats's *Ode to a Nightingale,* we could hardly have considered them for a prize when they were asked to discuss the fruitless knocking on a moonlit door of a midnight traveller concerned, directly or indirectly, with the wine trade, and to do it in the metre of Walter de la Mare's poem on the same subject. This isn't a difficult metre by any means; you can stuff any number of syllables into the odd lines, within reason, and you only have to rhyme on the even ones.

So out went, for example, one competitor's implication that the Dominic's are really Welsh—

'It's me, Dominic the Wine,' he cried
    despairingly.
      'Crackers are you inside there?
All this pretending you are not in look you—
    Open or miss it you will.'

Of those that remained, half-a-dozen or so
floated to the top like cream on a bottle of T.T.
milk. L. G. Begg provides an example of what
many competitors thought the explanation of
this curious encounter—
Never the least stir made the listeners
Though their consciences creaked like a
    board
As they thought of the order they'd given the
    traveller
For wines they could not afford:
Château Lafite by the magnum
Dom Perignon by the crate
Graacher Himmelreich Spätlese
And a tun of Fonseca '08.

Robert Gittings adds a touch of Cockaigne to
the same situation—
. . . For he suddenly smote on the door,
    crying
'These empties give you away.
We've let you have credit for fourteen years,
But now you've got to pay!'
Nothing stirred beyond the stout oak door,
Though his banging had loosened a chunk;
On the other side of it, stretched on the floor,
Lay the Customer—blissfully drunk.

J. H. Gooden got that moonlit door open,
though not by strictly mortal means—

Then he opened up the door, did the
    Traveller,
And moonlight flooded the floor;
He entered the room and the cobwebbed
    bottles
Were gray in the ghostly light—
'I have kept my word,' said the Traveller,
I have brought the case tonight'
And those words were the same that the
    Traveller had used
When he'd sold his wines alive.

The Traveller that R. H. G. Arnold sees was

not selling but buying, or rather failing to buy:

For of that famous vintage of Fifty-Three
Nothing remained in store,
And the host of the Château in despair
Would not even answer the door

So the traveller's dream of hogsheads to buy
Ended that dismal day
As he stabled his horse at the next auberge
And called for a vin du pays.

J. P. Ricks visualized beyond the door a
Merchant optimistically hoping for a wine that
M. André Simon tells us in *The Art of Good
Living* (the 1951 edition) is 'still firm, beautiful
of colour and bouquet, not showing any trace
of decay, but, unfortunately, very difficult to
find'—

Said the Merchant to his guests at the tasting
'They have sent no Latour '34.
I will go and search for the Traveller;
You listen for his knock at the door.'
Throughout the night the guests listened,
And tasted—drank—quaffed deep,
Till the candles guttered, and the listeners
Lay in unhearing sleep.

—and the Merchant, presumably, was still
worrying the Traveller for that claret that was
very difficult to find even thirteen years ago.
    Very pathetic is the tale told by R. S.
Stanier—

He was carrying a case of samples—
Sparkling, white, rosé and red—
And after his ride through the forest
They felt as heavy as lead.
The corkscrew burnt a hole in his pocket,
But he sadly resumed his course.
He'd have shared his last bottle with anyone,
But you can't sit and drink with a horse.

SUMMARY
*1st R. S. Stanier, Oxford, £15; 2nd. L. G. Begg,
Meopham, £10; 3rd. R. Gittings, Chichester,
£5. Consolatory bottles value 1 guinea to J. H.
Gooden, Bridport, J. P. Ricks, of Barnet, and
R. H. G. Arnold, of Folkestone.*

1965—WINE AND MUSIC This winter brought forth a Wine and Music number of WINEMINE and Spike Hughes suggested limericks, which he agreed to judge, on composers, assuming that they had devoted their lives exclusively to the wine trade, or in the case of a certain exception, to music. The choice was: Bach, Mozart, Caruso, Cole Porter, Callas, Bing Crosby, Louis Armstrong, Vera Lynn, the Beatles and Peter Dominic.

As so often with Christmas competitions of the kind many of the wittiest entries were also the bawdiest and therefore the unprintablest. But then perhaps this isn't really so surprising, since the limerick has long ceased to be the innocuous little jingle made famous, but not invented, by Edward Lear in his *Nonsense Poems* (1846). The first-known example of the limerick occurred in *Anecdotes and Adventures of Fifteen Young Ladies* and *History of Sixteen Wonderful Old Women,* both published in 1820 —curious surroundings, when one thinks of it, for the birth of an art-form which has become as much a masculine medium of self-expression as the latest Stock Exchange story (which, in my experience, it greatly surpasses in wit, point and the art of unembroidered narrative).

Perhaps because of its present and almost exclusive use by men, it was the women entrants for the competition who proved most shaky when it came to the form of the limerick. Some obviously did not know what a limerick was at all and submitted sycophantic quatrains praising Peter Dominic in the manner of TV commercials; others ignored the conventional rhyme-structure (not even in a Christmas competition can a judge's conscience be so full of seasonal goodwill as to allow 'imbibe' as a rhyme for 'carol'), while one composed a six-line stanza with the rhyme a,a,b,c,c,b. The classical metre of the limerick was also treated in rather cavalier fashion by women entrants. Several times the two feet of the third and fourth lines were stretched to fit the rhythm of 'Phil the Fluter's Ball'. Both sexes, on the other hand, were occasionally guilty of an archaic practice which, while technically permissible, is nowadays regarded by the true limericist as asking for anticlimax. This is the evasion of the pay-off in the last line by tamely repeating the first line with a very slight variation. Lear did it all the time; when a limerick began 'There was

86

an old person in black', he ended it with, 'That helpless old person in black'.

The number of entries—around 60—was small compared with other years, and the standard, I am afraid, was not very high. Perhaps, because the subject was musical there was a sad tendency to fill the verses with those inversions and perversions of the English language which abound in translations of opera librettos, where people say 'What from vengeance yet restrains me?'—even though the Italian translated literally comes out as, 'What holds me back?' (see the Sextet from *Lucia di Lammermoor*). One quite ingenious entry on Maria Callas was spoilt by a third line so inverted that one had to read it over again to find the subject and object of the sentence.

A vendeuse of wine from Aegea
Sipped a vintage from Pantellaria;
Her niece her espied
And said with some pride:
'Good gracious, it's Tia Maria!'

The greatest number of entries were inspired by Bach, whose name produced a crop of near-rhymes like Ark, lark, dark, mark, park, as well as some really unpermissible ones like sock, hock (to rhyme with lark in one case), sack and laugh. There were two extremely good Bach limericks, the first from Gordon Begg:

Johann Sebastian Bach
Kept a wine shop near Cardiff Arms Pach;
He supplied all the cafés
With wine for the tafés,
Then went home and wrote 'Sospan Fach'.

This, I thought was the best of the competition. It made me laugh; the story is neat and unexpected; it is full of local colour with neat puns and composed with an ingenious play on

Welsh words. For the benefit of those who do not know Wales or the Welsh—even from the radio or telly—the atmosphere of an international Rugby match in which Wales are playing, whether at Cardiff Arms Park, Twickenham, Dublin or Paris, I had better explain that 'Sospan Fach' means 'Little Saucepan'—

fach being a variant of the Welsh word *bach*, which means 'little'. Hence my delight in Mr. Begg's play on words. *Sospan fach* is traditionally one of the songs the Welsh sing at an international, or, indeed, in pubs after any Rugby game at all. It originated in Llanelly—or as it is now known again, Llanelli—the centre of the Welsh tinplate industry and is an affectionate little song about a saucepan set to a remarkably stirring tune. I know all this, not because I am Welsh, but because I spent too many winter Saturday afternoons when young in surroundings where I could never escape. I know I have a Welsh name; in fact, I am Irish—a circumstance which the Welsh recognise especially in Carnarvonshire where there are thousands of Hugheses, and where, when I explained this to him, Jones the post, who was also Jones the Pub, consoled me by saying, 'Well, never mind. We're all Celts'. Another entrant, W. J. Nott, also remembered that Bach was a composer and produced a nice twist with one of the few Bach limericks received that avoided having a rhyme for the composer's name:

Herr Bach, known from Dresden to China,
Owned a vineyard that could not be finer.
Frau B said 'I s'pose
A will you'll compose,
And leave all the lot to B, Minor?'

L. J. Allan, author of the Callas piece quoted above, also avoided awkward rhymes and introduced a musical allusion in his Bach limerick:

A vintner named Bach said 'I fear
This vintage is not a good year,
Although a bad taste
It needn't go waste—
T'will oil my well-tempered clavier'.

Mozart, like Bach, proved a stumbling block for many who tried to find rhymes for his name. E. Teskey-King was more cunning; he let Mozart's name look after itself and produced a real corker of a rhyme in two languages:

Vintner Mozart, when asked if he'd state
Why his life was so happy, said 'Mate!
I've a shop full of wine, a
Top Pop "Eine kleine
Nachtmusik", and Constanze to "date".'

The same competitor, E. Teskey-King, also produced a promising verse about Peter Dominic, but had to be disqualified for an outrageous final rhyme which can only be said to rhyme at all if it is grossly mis-pronounced or regarded as a purely visual thyme:

Peter Dominic's unusual flair
For composing light music was rare;
But his critics all froze
At the titles he chose,
Such as 'Riesling', 'Carafino', 'Cinque Terre'.

The author's own comment—'the last rhyme took some finding'—is understandable, and he might have got away with it, mispronunciation and all, if there hadn't been at least one legitimate rhyme that would have served his purpose—namely, 'Sancerre'.

The best of the Peter Dominic verses was John Flood's:

Peter Dominic, F.R.A.M.,
Conducted his own Requiem,
The theme of this opus
Was 'When you must drop us
Be sure it's at Château Yquem'.

Two entries which failed to confirm strictly
enough to the competition-setter's condition,
were both such good limericks in themselves
that I think they deserve to be rewarded with
consolatory bottles. The first by Lt. Col. R. K.
Spurrell, was certainly connected with Mozart,
but not with Mozart as a member of the wine
trade:

'Twas Leporello, the servant, who said:
'My master's not right in the head.
The appropriate manner
To woo Donna Anna
Is Carafino in litres in bed'

The other entry is from T. R. Alexander and
runs:

An Athenian merchant named Callas
Once put gin in a Catholic Chalice.
Said the Bishop of Thrake:
'Twas done by mistake,
And not out of Orthodox malice.'

The reason I do not think this qualifies is that
the mere mention of Callas is not enough to
make it a limerick about Callas as a wine
merchant. The limerick would not have lost its
point if the Athenian merchant had been
called Pallas, or Vallas or Thallas, or any other
Greek name that happened to rhyme (more or
less) with malice or chalice. The Bach and
Mozart verses tell us something of their
subjects; this one doesn't.

Callas did not prove so attractive a subject
as one might have expected; her name led to a
number of rhymes (Dallas and palace were the
most frequent) but for no particular reasons.
Vera Lynn and Caruso regularly suggested gin
and ouzo but little else; Louis Armstrong and
the Beatles inspired nothing that was relevant.
Cole Porter (he once wrote a song about the
Babes in the Wood who 'thought the Fountain
of Youth was gin and vermouth') suffered from

being invariably rhymed with daughter, but
neatly and to the point only by Mrs. C. J. C.
Manning:

A Hungarian nobleman's daughter
Fell madly in love with Cole Porter
He toiled night and day
Growing grapes for Tokay
Thus earning enough to support 'er.

THE AWARDS
*First prize £15 to Gordon Begg, London S.W.1
for his Bach.*
*Second prize £10 to E. Teskey-King, Hull for his
Mozart.*
*Third prize £5 to W. J. Nott, Barnstaple for his
Bach.*

At my request extra prizes of £3 in wine have
been awarded to John Flood, Hemel Hemp-
stead, for his limerick on Peter Dominic, L. J.
Allan, Watford, for his on Bach and Mrs. C. J.
C. Manning, Wilmslow, for hers on Cole
Porter.

Consolatory bottles to T. R. Alexander,
Shorne, Nr. Gravesend, for the limerick that
was almost about Callas and to Lt. Col. R. K.
Spurrell, Lingfield, for a limerick that could
change the whole plot of *Don Giovanni*.

Absolute Proof

Methods of measuring alcoholic strength vary from country to country and many people find them difficult enough to understand in their own. We can however start by agreeing that water (containing no alcohol) can be rated 0 at the bottom of any scale and that absolute alcohol will come at the top.

Between top and bottom, the scale can be divided up into any number of parts, just as a mile can be divided into yards, chains, furlongs or metres. In this case, the Americans divided their scale into 200 equal parts, the Europeans into 100 and the British into 175. The British were not just obtuse; they wanted proof spirit to be 100 on theirs.

Proof spirit had long been regarded as a roughly 50/50 mixture of absolute alcohol and water before Sikes' hydrometer provided the means of an accurate laboratory definition—a liquid which at 51° F. contains 57.06% alcohol by volume. For practical purposes, it was easier to let proof be represented by 100 and to refer to strengths as so much under or over Proof or so many degrees Proof, e.g. 30 under proof = 70° proof = $\frac{70}{175}$ parts of pure alcohol. The Excise measured the strength of home-made spirits in this way and the Customs naturally followed suit when demanding duty on imported wines.

'Proof', and dilution with water, were of no interest to Europeans, concerned principally with wine. They had adopted the scale of Gay-Lussac, a French physicist (1778–1850), which fixes Absolute Alcohol as 100°. A comparison between the two scales is made below but any number of degrees proof can be converted to degrees absolute by dividing by 7/4, e.g. 70° proof—40° absolute.

FRANCE—	TABLE WINES				VERMOUTH SHERRY PORT				SPIRITS		
DEGREES OF ABSOLUTE ALCOHOL	9	11	13	14	17	19	20	21	40	57·1	100
UK—DEGREES OF PROOF SPIRIT	15·9	19·4	23·1	26·4	29·9	33·4	35	37	70	100	175·1

The Americans also made proof spirit 100 on their scale but with 200 divisions their 'proof' works out at 100/200 or 50 per cent. absolute alcohol. Italy and Russia follow France but their volume calculations are based on a slightly different temperature. Germany prefers to ignore volume, measuring in degrees of absolute alcohol *by weight*. Fortunately none of this interferes with European drinking but what a lovely job lies in store for a keen Common Market co-ordinator!

DULCE ET DECORUM EST PRO PATRIA BIBERE

The wine-drinker's contribution per bottle to the Exchequer then and now:

	1960	
Champagne	4/3	
Sparkling Wines	4/3	7/5½
Foreign Table Wines bottled in UK	2/2	5/4½
Foreign Table Wines bottled abroad	2/7	5/9½
Commonwealth Table Wines	1/9	5/0½
Port, Sherry, Madeira	4/5	9/5½
Commonwealth Fortified Wines	2/8	7/4
Spirits and Liqueurs 70° Proof	25/6	44/–

**WineMine
A First Anthology**

PART THREE

WineMine and the Arts

Ben Nicholson, Auberge de la Sole Dieppoise 1932

Modern Artists and Drink

by Sheldon Williams

Bacchus and festive romps have been well-received subjects from painters and sculptors for centuries, but it really took the modern artists to get down to the idea of serious drinking.

Men like Toulouse-Lautrec gave a new Bohemian relish to the dreaded absinthe, and Degas recorded in terrifying realism the pathetic degradation that over-indulgence in the toxic green liquid could bring about. His painting of 'The Absinthe Drinkers' is enough to make the young student of the Arts teetotal for life. Picasso's bar habitués also showed signs of addiction, but the big buyers at today's auctions must sigh when they recall that Modigliani used to swap his exquisite drawings for a glass of wine.

It was the cubists who brought back the grape as an essential part of a modern picture. Their famous 'Still Life' paintings stuck to a short list of ingredients. A guitar, a bowl of fruit, a carton of cigarettes perhaps, but always a glass and a bottle of wine to go with it.

Cubism was essentially a product of France. The cubists painted a French way of life. They wanted to reflect a bourgeois existence. How better than with the French symbol of work and leisure—Wine!

Because they were turning conventional picture-making inside out, they needed to paint ordinary objects which, if not immediately recognisable, would soon rid the viewer of pre-conceived ideas just because what he was looking at—however distorted or bizarre—was basically familiar. Rather unfairly, unsophisticated gallery-goers of those pioneer days suggested that it was not so much theory that led to *four*-dimensional experiments in cubism, so much as liberal and perhaps unwise libations. Their philistine sniggers have a tragi-comic echo today, when cubist Still Life paintings (glasses, bottles and all) touch four- and five-figure prices at international art sales.

Do we sing only of the heroes of the past?

Today's painters and sculptors have been just as eager to demonstrate their affection for

Pablo Picasso, The Absinthe Drinker
Kunsthalle

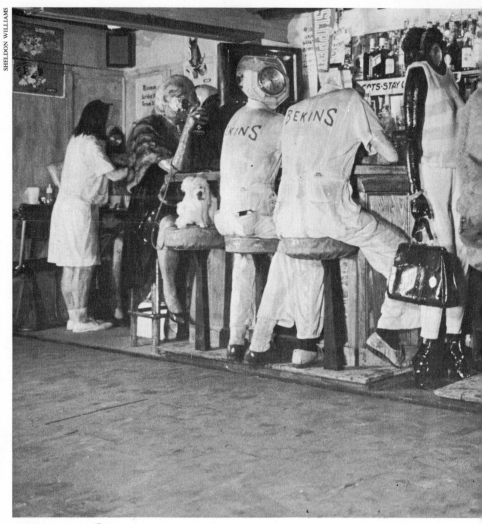

Edward Kienholz, The Beanery 1965. This awe-inspiring mixed media constituted the sole exhibit at the opening of the Dwan Gallery in New York. The figures are life size.

Pablo Picasso, Violin and bottle on a table.

the grape. Jean Lurcat, the acknowledged modern master of the art of tapestry, composed an awning of sumptuous splendour: 'Le Vin Bleu', in which three goblets, well-charged, are set in a bower of vine leaves and bunches of grapes lit by a rayed-sun and attended by butterflies of brilliant hue whose wings are fretted like the vine itself. Overhead, a bird is poised bill downwards ready to sup, while a less sober companion lies on its back, pinions outstretched, beak open, resting after its tipple. This is an important work—over a metre tall and nearly two metres wide.

Wine, a symbol of civilisation as vital as the wheel, gained a first place at the Pittsburgh International when Brianchon won the 'Garden Prize'. Its appearance as a subject for painting has international acceptance. It is as if, in a world of constant change, painters and aesthetes alike both see in the vineyard something permanent upon which they can base their trust. Wine's antiquity and its seasonal replenishment are an attraction to artists wherever the grape will grow. Braque, for instance, stepped aside from his intellectual exercises in cubism to paint a series of giantesses ('Caryatids' he called them) who carried platters of vintage grapes or bore upon their heads baskets of fruit ready for the wine-press. Dufy, surely the lightest and gayest amongst the moderns, loved the vineyards and would convey their loaded branches in bands of rich colour decorated with drawing (with the aid of a thin brush) or thousands of grapes ready for the harvest.

In such ways, wine has inspired the artist and brought happiness to his admirers. Such pictures are a far cry from the skid-row decrepitude of Degas' 'Absinthe Drinkers'. Yet every coin has its other side. There is no drama where the sun shines all the time and where there are no shadows.

Whatever the true facts behind the tragic relationship between Suzanne Valadon and her famous son Maurice Utrillo, the upshot has never been in doubt. Mlle. Valadon was a spirited woman, a peach of a model held in high esteem by all the painters of Paris. She was also—although this side of her nature did not manifest itself until later—a fine artist in her

Pablo Picasso, Still Life with Wine Glass

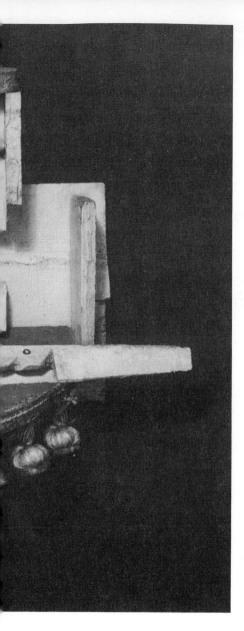

own right. It was her misfortune rather than design that all the men with whom she fell in love, failed to regularise their relationship with her. One of them, although it is by no means certain who, was the father of Maurice. M. Utrillo Snr., a person of no special account, merely agreed to give his name to the boy. Young Maurice Utrillo never seems to have had much to do with his 'surname father'. Instead all his affection was lavished upon his mother. As a token of the bond between them, he even signed his earliest canvases 'Maurice Utrillo V', a valuable source of information to art experts later when they came to date them.

Mlle. Valadon early realised the talent of her child and, it seems, decided to capitalise this unexpected vein of wealth. Almost simultaneously she appears to have recognised Maurice's weakness for the bottle. There are terrible stories—probably apocryphal—of how she kept him locked in with liquor and paints so that he could flood the art market of Paris (and later, the world) with his famous versions of the bainlieu of Montmartre. One thing is certain. By the time Maurice Utrillo managed to prise himself away from the influence of his mother and the ties of affection were finally loosed, he had become a slave to his glass of red wine. So much so that to meet its cost he found himself feverishly copying coloured postcards of Paris views to the consternation of his admirers and the destruction of his reputation amongst dealers and collectors. The story has a happy ending.

Utrillo was ultimately rescued from his plight—by marriage. His new wife completely altered his régime. She insisted on a balanced liquor consumption. Peace was restored, and Utrillo (having successfully sued the Tate Gallery for printing in their catalogue that he had died of drink) spent his remaining years quietly painting and restoring his position in the world of modern art to its previous eminence.

A salutary story—and one that shows that it *is* possible to overdo a good thing. Meanwhile, Paris and even New York (a latecomer in the list of world art centres) have taken second place to London as the international heart of the art market. Christie's and Sotheby's

Georges Braque, Still Life

thrive and each fabulous art sale adds to their respect in universal terms. The 180 art galleries of London have increased in number (and continue to do so almost weekly), and a new element has established itself in British art business—'The Private View'.

Of course, there is nothing new about 'private views', openings', 'vernissages' call them what you will. They have been part and parcel of the promotion of exhibitions and artists for decades. Today's difference is in their multiplicity.

In a full week, critics and clients can expect to be invited to anything from a dozen to twenty opening parties. Few can imagine putting in an appearance at all or even most of these, so the challenge of competition is strong. Obviously, galleries, if they are to use the opening of an exhibition as a magnet, will vie with each other not only to offer the finest picture fare, but also to charge glasses to their best advantage.

In the past few years, never has so much champagne been downed with such singleness of purpose. Galleries, which began by serving Algerian wine to their guests, have discovered that currently a falling off of enthusiasm can be directly attributable to 'gallery education' of artlovers' palates. So the quality—as well as the quantity—of consumption has gone up. The galleries, in fact, have been quite a contributary factor in the upsurge in wine by the British in general.

And the pictures . . . ? And the artists . . . ?

There has been a strong spate of buying. Recessions come and go, but artists have never known a more clement climate for painting and sculpture in Britain. The old spectre of the starving genius in a garret has been modified by extra income coming in from teaching jobs and cash prizes, scholarships and bursaries, but even without these supplements, art is flourishing.

Wine, which for so long has been an inspiration to painters and sculptors, is now seen to be playing a vital part at the crucial moment when a patron makes up his mind— 'Shall I, or Shan't I?'

Bacchus, long suspected of cultured tastes is shown in a new rôle—that of Entre-preneur!

101

A Too Comic Opera

by Jon Holliday

No one in his right mind expects overmuch realism in that hothouse world labelled 'Opera'—and this is illustrated in its wine-drinking as much as anywhere.

The big lady with the even bigger voice clutches what is obviously a papier-mâché goblet of purest gold, waves it dramatically all over the stage while she sings her way through a four-minute mile of trills, and then with one mighty quaff, empties the lot—at least one imperial pint of the stuff—down her throat.

To the innocent or the uninitiated this might seem like one of the occupational hazards of the job. Others who are certain that the goblet is empty, do not have any strong feelings on the subject—they do not expect the Tenor to get shot every performance, and by the same token, they do not expect the Soprano to get 'tiddly.'

Yet when I was in opera, we had *real* wine . . . with no disastrous results . . . well not what you could call *really* disastrous.

A company from La Scala Opera House in Milan had rather rashly ventured on a tour of the Australian capital cities. They brought a score of principals, conductors, stage directors, interpreters, and the like. But they had no chorus singers, no orchestra and no extras (supernumeraries—'walking ladies and gentlemen', to give them their old-fashioned title).

This is where I came in. I was young, fancy free, bone idle, and without funds. The Italians were offering 8s. 0d. a performance. They did eight shows a week, so that meant, if I could get into every performance, £3 4s. 0d. a week. This might not sound like Eldorado to you, but it was a magnificent sum to me.

Of course the thing to do was to get into all nineteen operas in the repertoire. *Aida* was fine because there were about 200 of us needed, to say nothing of the two camels, sundry dogs, and the elephant that never arrived from Sydney's Taronga Park Zoo.

All supers were on to a good thing with *Aida,* provided you did not mind blacking yourself all over (we were supposed to be Abyssinians—a likely story!) and then going home like that in the train, because there were no washing facilities for the humble supers.

At the other end of the scale, only two supers were needed for *Madame Butterfly.* By oriental cunning I managed to be one of them, thus ensuring that I missed none of the eight performances.

All went well until *Carmen,* which, apart from its musical merit and popularity, contains a glorious amount of wine drinking.

The Stage Director, who was a great admirer of the grape, did not believe that his cast should be 'fobbed off' with cochineal and water when the rich red products of his sun-soaked homeland vineyards were readily available. (Nobody drinks *white* wine on stage—white is theatrical symbolism for gin, and who has heard of an opera where the composer specified gin?)

In the tavern scene of *Carmen,* the performers were divided into four labels or classes. The principals drank Chianti in elegant glasses; the chorus a light table wine, not at all bad, in tumblers; the supers the cheapest rosso on the market, generously laced with the finest tap water; and the waiters 'lashings' of all three.

I was a waiter.

At least I *started* as a waiter. The trouble was that from the very first performance everyone developed a passion for the grape. There was something heady about drinking wine, even watered wine, in front of a packed audience, particularly as the issue was *free*.

The principals had to spend a lot of their energy during that scene wrestling their Chianti away from the chorus, who were trying to prevent all their table wine being 'swiped' by the supers, who were attempting without much success, to prevent the waiters from drinking all three.

By the time the dancers came on, *Carmen* was as merry as it was ever likely to be in the Southern Hemisphere. There was a vivacity about that opening performance which would have done Bizet a power of good if he had happened to drop in.

Needless to say things got out of hand, for the waiters were the only ones who had legitimate excuses to keep popping on and off stage and getting at the bottle store. I don't want to boast, but we also seemed able to drink faster.

This was our undoing. We never had any rehearsal. The Stage Director had just marched us around the stage before the curtain went up shouting: 'When she sit down, up you go. She sing, off you go. On when he come. I clap my hands, all off.'

I don't know what things are like at Covent Garden, but believe me, this theory of acting leaves a lot to be desired.

Without the wine it would have been difficult, perhaps impossible, to follow. With three free wines mixed indiscriminately, none of the waiters had any intention of following it. We just wandered around the stage drinking, until one teenage lad fell backwards off his chair in the middle of the Torreador song. I thought it added to the general gaiety, but the poor old Torreador was hopping mad. When he tried to down his Chianti at the end, it spluttered all over his shirt.

I did not let him have any more—in fact before the curtain came down the wine store had run dry!

The stage director had a few words to say, presumably on the qualities and the undoubted superiority of Italian wines (the word 'vino' kept getting mentioned) before sacking the lot of us.

Only when faced with the prospect of doing a 'crowdless' *Carmen*, did he relent. I even got my job back as a waiter, but there was not the same run on raspberry syrup as there had been on those dark succulent grape juices of the hot Italian hillsides.

Whenever I feel that whispering basket-like cover around a Chianti flask, my toast is always to *Carmen*. Now you know why.

Wine with Ballet

In the late summer of 1789 the Third Estate of the States-General debated the Rights of Man in Paris while the first moves were made to gather the vintage around Bordeaux. At that moment a ballet, *La Fille Mal Gardée,* added its mite to the storm convulsing France. This tale of a girl, who eludes her mother's watchful eye to marry the boy she loves, had been an immediate success when it was seen for the first time at the Grand-Théâtre, Bordeaux, on July 1. One reason for success was its down-to-earth humour and its setting in the familiar world of a French village, very different from the classical heroes and idealised rustics of earlier eighteenth-century ballet.

The performances at the Grand-Théâtre continued while Bordeaux, receiving the heady news from Paris, did all it could to encourage the cause of liberty on the Gironde. One evening ballet and revolution joined forces on stage. There is a scene at the end of the first act during which reapers in the fields break off to eat, drink and dance. Suddenly, as if spontaneously this evening, the principal dancer raised his glass and proposed a toast to the Third Estate. It was greeted with wild applause from the audience, who cheered again when the dancers sang topical verses as part of the finale to the ballet.

This incident was unearthed by Ivor Guest during research for Frederick Ashton's version of *La Fille Mal Gardée* which the Royal Ballet dance today at Covent Garden. There isn't a toast to the Third Estate in our version, but the reapers' picnic is still there and so is their singing when they leave the stage before the final curtain.

For myself I like to recall the ballet as it must have been at the Grand-Théâtre. If you know Bordeaux you will know the mellow stones of this theatre, classical, elegant, reflecting an eighteenth-century prosperity which owed less to wine, I admit, than to West Indian trade. Yet the Grand-Théâtre, which saw in *La Fille Mal Gardée* the first important ballet of modern times, becomes by its very situation a kind of symbol of what the stage owes the vine. Our less inhibited forefathers in the Hellenic beginnings of our world gave the vine full credit for its liberating influence upon the human spirit. Out of their annual celebration of the vintage grew the theatre. And before the priest of Dionysus, god of wine, the theatre's early works were offered for the first time.

All this may seem a long way from Giselle's gentle steps, or the diamond brilliance of a modern ballerina. Yet the dance, the most immediate and elemental of human responses, is linked more than other kinds of theatre to the Dionysian rites. Ballet acknowledges this in the frequent use it makes of wine and wine harvests as an excuse for dancing. One of the most effective pieces in the new version of *Swan Lake* at Covent Garden, for instance, is Rudolf Nureyev's Polonaise for the court, which begins with a toast to the Prince. So, too, raised goblets launch the dances at the Capulet Ball in the Bolshoi's *Romeo and Juliet*.

Giselle and *Coppelia* go further because both of them actually take place at harvest time. In *Coppelia* at Covent Garden we miss a trick by not emphasising this season as the Danish Ballet do, giving the celebrations at the end of the story more character. In *Giselle* we have taken the cue and restored the scene where Giselle is crowned Queen of the Vintage as she was at the first production in 1841. Compare photograph and print! The two are almost identical.

Coppelia being set in Galicia I suppose the

Elizabeth Anderton as Giselle in the Covent Garden production.

villagers and even old Doctor Coppelius himself would drink something like Janos Riesling or Egri Bikaver. If they were in the money they might have chosen Lenz Moser's Schluck or Blue Danube from Austria, especially since Moser's way of growing grapes has improved the wine a good deal since *Coppelia* first appeared in 1870.

Giselle lived in Thuringia. I don't know Thuringian wines but I guess them to be light and short-lived. The local Duke, whose son caused Giselle all her troubles, should have preferred Goethe's Steinwein. After all, it was German literature which created him by inspiring Goethe.

There are about twenty ballets from the current repertoire on my list all of which include wine somewhere in their action. There are many, many more in history. The most human I think, belongs to Fokine, the great choreographer of Diaghilev's Ballets Russes. His first work in 1906 as a young man in St. Petersburg was called *La Vigne* and represented the characteristics of various wines through dancing. It's an idea someone might follow again today. He chose his dancers very carefully and cast the sparkling, high-spirited Lydia Kyaksht as Champagne. To represent bubbles and foam he made her rise through a trap-door *already spinning on pointe*. It must have been tricky and frightening. But it worked. I drink to her when I drink Champagne.

Giselle by Jean Coralli and Jules Perrot, Paris, 1841. Giselle is crowned Queen of the Wine Harvest.

If only they could play . . .

by Ernest Atkinson

My attempt to write about the addiction to the pleasures of wine of the clergy, the lesser clergy, and various humbler if not less vocal servants of the Church, the musicians, the organ blowers, the vergers, the sextons and all the the rest turns out to be less easy than expected.

The topic is not quite so well documented as one may be apt to suppose. Or so I think. There is a kind of folklore about the monks who slept all the day and who drank all the night which gave a start to one Rugby football club singing piece I used to know, I have found also in *The British Minstrel,* published in 1827, a song to be sung by a sexton, who, if I read the text rightly, had buried no fewer than four of his wives:

> . . . From earth and air I earn my bread,
> By my spade and my birds so gay.
> My fire of youth is gone and fled,
> And water's too cold for me:
> So I'm forc'd to drink good wine instead.
>   Heigho! fol de riddle dol de.

> To three fair maids, as blithe as May,
> In wedlock was I bound:
> One scolded, one tippled, and one ran away,
> But I popped 'em all in the ground.
> A fourth I tried, which lovely bride,
> Beat all the other three;
> She'd have beat me, too—but alas she died.
>   Heigho! fol de riddle dol de.

Or there is another one:

> A plague upon parsons and preachers,
> And all this palavering shew,
> Why, what in God's name can they teach us,
> But what we all knew long ago.

> There is but little sin I believe,
> In glasses, in girls, or in rhymes;
> If our crimes, too, make nobody grieve,
> Why we never need grieve for our crimes.

> Then drink away, drown care and sorrow,
> Let your eyes and your glasses be bright,
> We all may be buried tomorrow,
> So let us be happy tonight.

All of which may be good nineteenth century balladry, if not very good doctrine.

There is a kind of antiphony, related to our present theme, over the Battle of Hastings. There were Harold's men drinking the night heartily away and singing songs they had a mind to; while William's men were singing litanies and making their confessions. Or so it is

108

recorded by William of Malmesbury. A much later historian, Augustin Thierry, says that while the Normans were polishing up their armour and sharpening their weapons, the men of religion were at liturgical music and other appropriate exercises.

'In the other army, William writes, 'The night went by in very different style; entirely taken up with patriotism and full of a self-confidence that the outcome of the morrow would belie, the Saxons enjoyed themselves with a great deal of noise, singing old national songs (whatever indeed those may have been) emptying, the while, around their camp fires horns of wine and of beer.' The beer we can imagine. What the wine may have been I, for one, cannot.

A later generation, I daresay, first heard that near-devout Latin song, 'Meum est propositum in taberna mori'. I find, well-nigh forty years on, in the blank pages at the end of my copy of the *Week End Book,* a sober attempt of my own to put music to this. I rather fancy that it owed something to echoes of the music I was mainly concerned with at the time as a church organist at no less than £30 a year. I dare not claim any originality for it. There is probably something very like it in the Rouen Church Melodies.

But it goes thus:

Meum est propositum
In taberna mori
Vina sit appositum
Morentis ori

Ut dicant cum venerit
Angelorum chori

'Deus sit propitius
Huic potatori'

Skip a few hundred years and move up, I daresay, in the social scale. There was Parson Woodforde, for example. At Oxford around 1760 he was cheerfully recording that he was being dunned for wine debts from Hartley and Robinson of Southampton 'for £8 15s. 0d. for half a hogshead of old Port, that I had from Southampton last year'. It looks as though he might have been disciplined a little for this for on Christmas Eve he records he paid the money 'through Mr. Pryor our College Steward'. One may suppose that he sang in Chapel the next morning with cheerfuller voice knowing that that was off his mind. (Later, by the way, he borrows £250 to pay off his Oxford debts). Anyway in college he drank a great deal of wine. When he was made a Fellow of New College in 1761 he treated the Bachelors' Common Room 'all the evening with wine and punch'. It was not the only occasion of the kind.

In that same year, November 4th, he records: 'Dyer laid Williams 2s. 6d. that he drank 3 pints of Wine in 3 hours, and that he wrote 5 verses of the Bible right,' but he lost.

He did it in the B.C.R., he drank all the Wine, but could not write right for his life. He was immensely drunk about 5 Minutes afterwards.'

He was ordained Deacon on the morning of May 29th, 1763, and notes: 'We were in C.Church Cathedral from nine o'clock this morning till after twelve. For wine this afternoon in the B.C.R. pd. 0.0.6.'

As to drinking habits, he seems to have been learning. On 'Septem.7 . . . Had three bottles of Wine out of my room in ye B.C.R. this afternoon and Waring had another out of his room. Waring was very drunk and Bedford was little better. N.B. I was very sober, as I had made a resolution never to get drunk again, when at Geree's rooms in April last, when I fell down dead, and cut my Occiput very bad indeed'.

What is a little puzzling is that later on, when he gets to his East Anglian parish in which he wrote the diary that engages our minds still so much today he buys so much wine, and brews so much beer, and takes into his household so much gin and suchlike, yet makes little record of how it comes to be enjoyed. He gives gin and rum and beer away to his servants and the poorer parishioners,

and to all comers on great occasions. This is all nicely recorded.

He records also splendid meals. It seems to have struck him as a little out of the ordinary, but it was not in fact greatly out of line with the daily fare of his household, when a friend sent word that he would like to take a Family Dinner. It gave Parson Woodforde's household a little disturbance but they fared thus:

'We gave the Company for dinner some Fish and Oyster Sauce, a nice Piece of Boiled Beef, a fine Neck of Pork rosted and Apple Sauce, some hashed Turkey, Mutton Stakes, Sallad, &c., a wild Duck rosted, fryed Rabbits, a plumb Pudding and some Tartlets. Desert, Some Olivers, Nutts, Almonds, and Raisins and Apples.'

But not a word about the wine. We can pick here and there in the Diary, and undoubtedly a handsome quantity of wine was being drunk, but the Parson does not mention it very significantly. But it is certainly there about the house or parsonage.

From one real, very real and human parson let us turn to the fictional, but perhaps not all that fictional, Reverend Doctor Middleton in *The Egoist*. Here was a man to enjoy his

water-drinker. And his father died early.

Pass over the harmonious details of the meal and the wines. Afterwards: A fresh decanter was placed before the doctor.

He said: 'I have but a girl to give'. He was melted.

'Sir Willoughby replied: 'I take her for the highest prize this world affords.'

Again, I am not quite sure how much that distinguished scene has to do with the behaviour of churchmen, distinguished or modest, in face of wine. But let us get back to the modest men. There is a charming little fable by Ivan Andreyevich Krylov, who wrote these things in verse early last century. They were translated, somewhat freely, I suspect, by Professor Bernard Pares in this century and published here first by Capes and then by Penguins.

We are back on the village musician and choirman level:

John Smith invited Jones to dinner.
'T'was not to keep his friend from growing thinner
But something else, you'll understand;
He wanted Jones to hear the village band.

The Village Band struck up—too sharp, too flat, no matter:
They made the roof resound.
Jones felt his ears splitting with this clatter,
His head went whirling round.

'Excuse me, Smith', said he, 'I'll eat my hat
If I can stand much more of that.
Your village band this afternoon
Is mercilessly out of tune;
They set my teeth on edge.'

'Well, yes,' said Smith, with feeling in his tone,
I'm bound to own
They're not musicians highly skilled,
But all are members of the Parish Guild,
And all have signed the Pledge.

'But as for me, I'd let them drink all day,
If only they could play'.

wines. Meredith must have had a nice taste himself, to look at this. What effect it may have had on the generous exercise of Dr. Middleton's ecclesiastic duties I would not venture to say, but, says Meredith, 'The hard labour of the day approved the cooling exercise, and the crowning refreshments of French cookery and wines of known vintages'.

But the Reverend Doctor was outplayed by Sir Willoughby Patterne. They had been to the cellars:

'I am going down to my inner cellar'.

'An inner cellar!' exclaimed the Doctor.

'Sacred from the butler. It is interdicted to Stoneman. Shall I offer myself as a guide to you? My cellars are worth a visit.'

'Cellars are not catacombs. They are, if rightly constructed, rightly considered, cloisters, where the bottle meditates on joys to bestow, not on dust misused; Have you anything great?'

'A wine aged ninety'.

'Is it associated with your pedigree, that you pronounce the age with such assurance?' (Note the early winemanship here.)

'My grandfather inherited it'.

And it turned out that his grandfather was a

Wine and Operetta

by Mark Lubbock

'Fill every glass
For wine inspires us
And fires us
With courage, love and joy
Women and wine
Should life employ
Is there aught else on earth desirous?
Fill every glass
For wine inspires us
And fires us
With courage, love and joy.'

Here is a splendid example of wine and operetta from the 18th century. *'The Beggars' Opera'* with *Macheath* and his highwaymen, *Lucy, Polly, John Gay's* expressive lyric and a fine tune, taken from a French drinking song, *'Que chacun remplisse son verre'*, from *Thomas D'Urfey's* collection of early 18th Century popular tunes called *Wit and Mirth,* or *Pills to Purge Melancholy.*

Ideally, Operetta should, in my opinion, be an amalgam of Wine, Women and Song and, incidentally, it is surprising to find that the well-known phrase, *Wine, Women and Song,* was coined by no less a person than the great religious reformer, *Martin Luther,* when he wrote: *'Wer nicht liebt Wein, Weib und Gesang, Der bleibt ein Narr sein Lebelang'.* *('Who loves not Wine, Women and Song, remains a Fool his whole life long'.)*

As I was saying, *Operetta* should be an amalgam of Wine, Women and Song. For wine is the perfect prelude to the subsequent enjoyment of women and song in *operetta.* I proved this as a young man when on a sum-

Kenneth Rowland as Macheath in a San Francisco performance of *The Beggars' Opera.*

112

mer's evening in 1924 at Salzburg after a delicious meal of salmon-trout and a bottle of *Graacher Domprobst,* I attended an exquisite performance of Johann Strauss's operetta, DIE FLEDERMAUS (1874).

Lotte Lehmann was *Rosalinde,* Elizabeth Schumann *Adele* and Richard Tauber *von Eisenstein.* The conductor was Bruno Walter. This is a memory to be treasured and I am sure that the wine contributed as much to my enjoyment in the auditorium as it added to the complications of the plot on the stage. For in no operetta does wine play such a significant rôle as it does in *Fledermaus.*

In the first act, in an intimate situation, *Rosalinde's* lover, The Tenor *Alfred,* is discovered drinking wine with her, *en déshabille* by the Prison Governor, *Herr Frank,* when he arrives to escort *Rosalinde's* husband, *Herr von Eisenstein,* to prison, *(von Eisenstein* has been sentenced to a short term of imprisonment for striking a policeman). *Alfred,* who cannot disclose his identity without compromising *Rosalinde,* is perforce removed to prison. Later that evening, *Herr von Eisenstein* who should have reported to the prison to start his sentence, is enjoying himself at *Prince Orlofsky's* party and, excited by the champagne he has drunk, is flirting with a beautiful Hungarian countess, who is wearing a mask. Behind the mask he fails to recognise his own wife and when he offers to count her heartbeats with his repeater watch, *Rosalinde* manages adroitly to purloin the watch's valuable evidence of her husband's faithlessness.

In addition to these two situations, most of the Finale to Act II is concerned with wine. By now the champagne has had its effect and *Prince Orlofsky's* guests are feeling mellow. All join in praise of champagne, The king of wines, and the whole company, glass in hand, swears eternal brotherhood and sisterhood. In the last act misunderstandings are cleared up. *Rosalinde's* possession of *von Eisenstein's* watch is compensated for by the presence in prison of *Rosalinde's* lover, the tenor *Alfred,* arrested while masquerading as her husband. As *von Eisenstein* philosophically declares, it's best to blame it all on the champagne.

In another Johann Strauss operetta, '*The Gipsy Baron*' (1885) recently revived at *Sadler's Wells,* wine is used as a recruiting earnest. Colonel *Homonay,* an Hungarian officer, is recruiting volunteers for the Spanish-Hungarian war in the 18th Century and the recruit instead of receiving the Queen's shilling is given a glass of recruiting wine.

Turning to French operetta, wine on the stage is usually associated with some scandalous goings-on—to precipitate an orgy or to make an individual drunk for some nefarious purpose. In Offenbach's *La Vie Parisienne* (1866) the composer and his librettists get a lot of fun out of the topic of fleecing the unwary tourist. A rascally guide manages to insinuate himself with a wealthy Swedish Baron, who is visiting Paris. Learning that the Baron desires to mix in Parisian high life, the guide borrows the drawing-room in a house belonging to the aunt of a friend of his, who is conveniently absent, and stages a bogus reception. The aunt's butler, footman, parlourmaid and the porter's six nieces are all dressed up to represent the guests and are presented to the Baron as various Princes, Generals, Viscountesses and Marquises. The Baron is enchanted. This is really seeing life. The climax of the evening is reached with the serving of supper and the Champagne produces an atmosphere of sheer delirium. The curtain falls on Act III of *La Vie Parisienne* to one of Offenbach's most rapturous melodies: 'Tout tourne, Tout danse'.

In Louis Varney's operetta *Les Mousquetaires au Couvent* (1880) which had a recent revival in Paris at the *Théâtre Gaîté-Lyrique,* two young Captains of Musketeers, *Gontran de Solanges* and *Armand de Brissac,* disguised as monks, present themselves at a convent where their girl friends, Marie and Louise, are at school. They inform the Mother Superior that they have called at the convent at the instigation of the governor of Touraine but their real purpose is to abduct their girls. The Mother Superior invites *de Brissac* to give the girls a religious address and he agrees. Unfortunately he discovers a bottle of brandy in the cellars of the convent and lurches into the schoolroom quite drunk. In spite of his brother officer's efforts to dissuade him, he insists on addressing the school and when the Mother

Superior arrives with the girls he scandalises everybody by preaching a most unsuitable sermon, glorifying Love:

'Aimons nous, aimons nous donc,
Telle est mon prèche
Qui n'aime pèche,
Aimons nous, aimons nous donc,
De cupidon vive la flèche.'

The Mother Superior and the nuns are affronted, but the girls, enchanted by the gaiety of the sermon and the preacher, leap to their feet dancing hilariously round *de Brissac* as the curtain falls on a scene of pandemonium.

Turning now to England, there are several intriguing and unexpected references to the effect of wine in operetta.

In *Gilbert and Sullivan's Trial by Jury* (1875) the trial of a suit for Breach of Promise, the defendant, a young man, who is being sued, tells the Court that he is not the man to make a girl happy:

'I smoke like a furnace—I'm always in Liquor;
A Ruffian, a bully, a sot.
I'm sure I should thrash her, perhaps I should kick her,
I am such a very bad lot.'

The Jury find the case a most puzzling one and apply to the learned Judge for guidance. He counsels them as follows:

'The question, Gentlemen, is one of liquor;
You ask for guidance—This is my reply:
He says when tipsy he would thrash and kick her
Let's make him tipsy, Gentlemen, and try'.

Counsel for the Plaintiff:
'With all respect
I do object.'
Defendant:
'I don't object.'
All:
'We do object.'

Their objections infuriate the Judge, who tosses his books and papers about, declaring that no proposals seem to please the Court and that he is not going to hang about all day. With startling suddenness he finishes the case with the words:

'Put your briefs upon the shelf,
I will marry her myself'.

In *Gilbert and Sullivan's Princess Ida* (1884) we have an example of wine giving the show away.

Three young men, *Hilarion, Cyril* and *Florian,* disguise themselves as girls and penetrate into *Princess Ida's* University for Women. They apply to be allowed to join and are received into the University as girl graduates in all good faith. A picnic lunch is served and unfortunately *Cyril,* who partakes too freely of the wine, becomes rather rowdy and obstreperous, to the manifest disapproval of *Princess Ida.* In spite of attempts by *Hilarion* and *Florian* to stop him, he insists on singing a most unsuitable song about kissing:

'Kiss me, kiss me, kiss me, kiss me,
tho' I die of shame-a
Please you, that's the kind of maid
sets my heart a-flame-a

Cyril's infamous behaviour provokes a quarrel among the young men and it quickly becomes apparent that these are no girls. *Princess Ida* will have no mercy on 'men in women's clothes' and in punishment for their sacrilegious intrusion, *Hilarion* and his two friends are bound by girl attendants and led away.

I always have a soft spot for *Madame Drivelli* in *J. T. Tanner* and *Adrian Ross's* 'Musical Play', *The Circus Girl* (1896), with music by *Ivan Caryll* and *Lionel Monckton.*

Madame Drivelli has grown too fat to be a circus performer and complains bitterly of her husband's neglect.

'Tho' I never like to make a fuss,
Unless a thing is positively shady,
But he never even paid
For a port and lemonade
And you can't do less than that to treat a lady.'

Die Fledermaus, Johann Strauss. 'Most of the finale to Act II is concerned with wine'.

Looking back on many hours spent in the musical theatres of London, Paris, Vienna and Berlin (both as a member of the audience and as a performer), memories of Wine and Operetta crowd back into my mind: Princess Marie's charming Rhine Waltz-song, glorifying The Rhine, its vineyards and its wine in Karl Zeller's DER VOGELHAENDLER (The Birdseller) (1891). More Offenbach memories; The disgraceful behaviour of the carbiniers in LES BRIGANDS (1869) who get drunk and, instead of protecting the Princess of Granada and her suite, whom they are supposed to be escorting to Mantua for the Princess's marriage to the Duke of Mantua, fraternise with the brigands, who intend to pillage the Spaniards. Then there are those two charming, amorous street-singers, Piquillo and Perichole, in LA PERICHOLE (1868), who are brought together in holy matrimony only by the generous libations of Champagne provided by the Viceroy of Peru; though the sequel to the marriage does not work out at all to his advantage as he schemed it should. Finally a café in Vienna in Noel Coward's BITTER SWEET (1929) with *Lieutenant Tranisch,* the possessor of a ringing baritone voice, rendering, with chorus of Officers the stirring song:

TOKAY ...
The golden sunshine of a summer's day.

All of which leaves me without the slightest doubt that wine has contributed not only to the gaiety of nations but much to the charm of Operetta.

RODNEY SYMES

Lord Lapper-Litre at The Theatre

by Donovan Kelly

It was in the great hall of Swillings Castle that we were privileged to hear Lord Lapper-Litre expound his theories about the Theatre; for which, it transpired, he had no kind of sympathy. 'Damn it all,' he explained, leaning against the massive Jacobean chimney-piece, above which the Lapper-Litre Arms (argent, four glasses gules) glowed in the evening light, 'Never go there if I can help it—sheer waste of time. All these play-writing fellows are unmitigated pussy-foots: they use wine to raise a cheap laugh, or worse still, to point an Awful Warning. You and I, my dear fellow, know that it's neither. Besides there's always too much play and too little interval. Hours and hours of talk and they expect a man to refresh for the next stretch in a crowded Bar.

The sole exception to his strictures was Glyndebourne, where, he conceded, they are civilised. There he was wont to pass the first hour notwithstanding the music, in happy anticipation of the Richebourg, Mouton or Vollrads he had already selected with care and to which he would soon be able to give an hour and a quarter of leisurely appreciation. So soothed, the rest of the evening would pass in a haze of gratified satisfaction, impenetrable to even the high C's of a well-meaning, and hard-working soprano.

The cause of our discussion was that at our earnest recommendation he had been to see a play. A very good play, we thought, but he could find nothing in it to admire. It was, he said, far too long—four hours, with only one brief bar-trekking interval. There were, to be sure, not wholly uncomplimentary references to wine, and the drinking of a health was accompanied by ornate ceremonies in which bands played and a gunfire salute marked the stately festivity of the occasion. There was a regal display of gilded paste-board goblets, in which his Lordship took considerable interest, until the unfortunate author committed the unpardonable solecism of making the mightiest and most magnificent goblet of all the vehicle for an extremely efficient poison.

'Enough to make a fellow fight shy of a glass,' said Lord Lapper-Litre with a snort. 'He's as bad as the rest of them—always down on wine. And those characters—a neurotic young fellow always talking to himself, a trollop, a murderer, a half-witted girl and a sententious old busybody; sheer torture to make a man listen to them—unfortified.'

Thinking over our friend's criticism we

came to the reluctant conclusion that playwrights viewed the grape with a jaundiced eye. Nor is that view a particularly English one. An obvious and depressing moral usually follows even a modest indulgence and in England an additional hurdle was raised by the Actor Managers, who found a drunken scene as essential as a bout of (melodic) madness to many 19th century operatic heroines. David Garrick—Wyndham, and Sidney Carton—Martin Harvey all jerked tears and laughter when in their stage cups. The tradition was carried on (and greatly ennobled) when Juno Boyle rose to a pinnacle of questioning integrity in the ruins of a whisky and stout sodden home.

The drawing-room comedy of Edwardian times was safe (and so 'naice') only as long as tea was dispensed, but real drama lurked uncomfortably near whenever a wine glass appeared. Villains drank spirits and when the feminine lead sipped champagne, a fate worse than death lurked behind the lath and canvas door.

We looked along our library shelves in an endeavour to find a play to suit Lord Lapper-Litre. Ben Jonson seemed a comparatively safe choice; neither overt nor implicit criticism of the liquors of the 'Mermaid' Tavern sours the splendid fun of 'Bartholomew Fair'. Only his regrettable advice to drink 'only with thine eyes' could be considered a black mark against him. But the contemporary Theatre has, seemingly, no place for his full-blooded, roistering and incredibly learned comedies, otherwise we might be joining his Lordship at a performance of 'Eastward Ho'.

The Scandinavian and Russian dramatists rarely allow any liquid refreshment to cheer the dismal business of living. In 'The Wild Duck' poor Hedvig's not over glamorous offer of a bottle of beer fails to raise Hjalmar from his self-induced misery, and when the champagne cork pops in the rain-drenched murk of 'Ghosts', the less discussable perversions and practices open grimly before us. Hedda Gabler's wish to see vine leaves in Lovberg's hair is a harbinger of particularly squalid DOOM. Yet the severe Ibsen, responsible for many such jaundiced incidents, also wrote the most theatrically effective drinking scene on the stage.

In 'Lady Inger of Ostraat' set in 16th century Norway, Lady Inger sits in her remote, gloomy castle, spinning, spiderlike, involved webs of political intrigue to the end of ridding the country of a foreign yoke. The times are harsh, dangerous and ruthless: there was only one forfeit for a political mistake: a forfeit exacted and paid on the headsman's block. Knowing this, Lady Inger, with the bravery born of fanaticism, pursues her course—trusting no one—proving and probing all. A mysterious messenger is expected to whom vital news is to be imparted: news that would be a death warrant in the wrong hands. In her isolation she has to rely upon her own wits to assess his reliability, and as she weighs her problem, not one, but two messengers are announced. Which, if either, can she trust? With gracious dignity she proffers them wine, presenting two flagons with stately ceremonial, bidding them 'Drink deep'. They do so, and she then tells them that the draughts were not identical: that in one was wine for her friend, in the other poison for her enemy. Their reactions are instant. 'Ah! I am poisoned,' cries one, and 'Death and damnation, you have murdered me!' the other. She knows what she needed to know, and that both are false. A thrilling *coup de Théatre;* we know of none more so.

Lord Lapper-Litre's reaction was a snort. 'Just like a woman to use wine for a shabby trick like that,' he commented indignantly.

Our talk wound back to Shakespeare. We said much in praise of that industrious playwright and conscientious drinker: quoted Falstaff's eulogy and remembered that wit and hard drinking went hand in hand. We recalled the apocryphal cause of his fatal illness, but our pleadings failed to win a favourable verdict.

'Can't stand the fellow,' said that ornament of the Upper House—'he's as bad as the rest of them; all pussyfoots, to a man. Come to think of it he wrote that awful play you advised me to see—called "A Village" or something like that.' It was with some diffidence that we suggested that the correct title was 'Hamlet'.

JOHN MASON

Lord Lapper-Litre, I suppose, did as much for Peter Dominic as the St. Bernard for Hennessy. He was always topically active on the back cover of Wine Mine, discovering a cask tapper and serious leakage in his cellar during the spy disclosures of 1963, sailing the Atlantic single-handed in 'The Pitcher' in 1965 and sitting up in his four poster bed at Christmas (wearing a night-cap of course) hemmed in, or sewn up, by all manner of liquors.

—*Editor*

121

WineMine
A First Anthology

PART FOUR

WineMine Abroad

The Festival of Saint Dominic

by Father Adolfo Angelucci, Parish Priest of Cocullo
Translation from the Italian by Joan Hogg

Hagiology played no part in the naming of Peter Dominic; it just happened over a game of dominoes. Nevertheless, a reference in Gordon Cooper's book *Festivals of Europe* to the Festival of St. Dominic at Cocullo led to Father Angelucci telling the story.

In this Parish there is a traditional religious festival which takes place on the first Thursday of May in honour of Saint Dominic, and our procession is perhaps the most characteristic in the entire Catholic Church.

In the first days of spring, when wild-life awakes from hibernation, groups of young men and boys set out in search of snakes, returning from the countryside to offer them to St. Dominic on his feast day.

The tradition has a Roman pagan origin. The Romans settled in this district to conquer Corfinium, about 50 kilometres from Cocullo, and the local people absorbed various Roman customs; for example, in the first days of May they offered homage to the Goddess Ancizia with live serpents to appeal for her favour and protection.

In 1000 A.D., St. Dominic was hiding from heretical persecution at Villalago, about 15 kilometres from Cocullo. The people were very poor, without shelter, and the womenfolk subject to snake bite. The snakes, having sucked their breasts dry of milk, then penetrated through the mouth into their stomachs. St. Dominic miraculously cast them out and cured the bites.

There are stories of his other miracles too. The wolf which returned the child to its mother; the poor woman who gave him some of her flour and received more; the poor peasant whose crops prospered after hiding the saint and the mule whose lost shoe was found. Many monasteries were built in the Abruzzi in the name of St. Dominic, and the pagan tradition of offering snakes to the goddess, Ancizia, passed on, with the authority of the Church, to him.

This tradition has been scrupulously maintained to the present day by the people of Cocullo. Today, the first Thursday in May, brings a great crowd of pilgrims, not only Italians but foreigners from both sides of the Atlantic and Sound and Television recorders too. Throughout the year come pilgrims to the sanctuary to ask for favours and to give presents in gratitude to the saint for his protection from snake-bite, rabies, hydrophobia and toothache! Among the many national monuments in the sanctuary is a hand-made silver relic of his Holy Molar which, according to history, he gave to the people of Cocullo before ascending into heaven.

On the morning of the festival, after a solemn Mass in his honour, comes the traditional procession of the Serpents. Outside the church the procession forms up. His statue is taken to the entrance of the sanctuary and upon it is placed the biggest and most beautiful of all the snakes. The procession then winds over the entire countryside.

And that, in a nutshell, is the festival of St. Dominic, which has now achieved universal fame through the press of many countries. The big dailies have written about us, the weeklies show photographs of our traditional event. Now—and not the least—comes WINEMINE, seeking too that fascination and attraction, which St. Dominic imparts in all our hearts.

125

The Phylloxera Story

by George Ordish

That great eighteenth-century introducer of plants to Britain, Phillip Miller, was more fortunate than his Victorian successors for he introduced few pests and diseases with the many thousands of species he imported.

In the mid-nineteenth century every gentleman and every rising industrialist had to have his conservatory and the world was ransacked for *exotica* with which to fill them. Of course at the same time there was a genuine scientific interest in plants: though there was but little appreciation of ecology. In fact the word was not invented until 1859, by Haeckel. As a result some devastating pests were carried around the world with the plants destined for display or study.

Among the plants which were to suffer in this way was the vine—the European vine, *Vitis vinifera*. Vines were successively attacked and almost wiped out by American pests: the powdery mildew from 1845, the *Phylloxera* from 1863 and the downy mildew from 1882. All these troubles were overcome by the exercise of human ingenuity and *Vitis vinifera* now flourishes the world over.

The phylloxera aphid was first remarked in Europe in a vinery at Hammersmith in 1863: it was studied by Professor I. O. Westwood at Oxford, who hesitated to name it, because he could find no males.

At about the same time the insect was getting to work in France, but it was not recognized as an insect: it was thought to be a disease. The attacked vine sickened, changed colour, made poor growth and eventually died. At that time the disease of consumption was a scourge of the human race and as the vines turned pale and sickened in the same way as did a consumptive patient, and died after two or three years of attack, the disease was called *étisie* after the *phtisie* of humans.

In France the trouble continued to spread and the *Gardeners' Chronicle and Agricultural Gazette* repeatedly kept its readers informed, by means of its reporters there and its extracts from the French press. Vine growers began to get alarmed: they remembered that the mildew had nearly extinguished the grapes in the 1840s and here was another threat yet more sinister and mysterious, for there was no apparent causal agent. The most strange and extraordinary reasons were advanced as a cause of the 'unknown disease,' such as the weather, a blight in the atmosphere and God's punishment for the country's abandonment of the Emperor.

French scientists started to study the trouble; unfortunately they did not know of Westwood's pioneer work in 1863. S. E. Planchon, sitting in his laboratory, somewhat in the manner of Mycroft Holmes, argued that, judging by the reports of the way the disease spread, something organic was the cause. With two colleagues (MM. Bazille and Sahut) he visited an attacked vineyard and in two days the team had uncovered the reason for the death of the vines—the attacks of the vine louse, or root aphid.

Nevertheless, in spite of this triumph the *Gardeners' Chronicle* rather felt that the English work had been neglected. In 1870 (p. 1212) it was stated: 'The French writers seem entirely to ignore the circumstances that the insect was described by Professor Westwood and Mr. Berkeley in our columns and that the identity of the insect on the leaf with that on the roots was established as long ago as 1867 by Professor Westwood.' Having discovered the cause, the next thing was to find a cure. Two fundamentally different methods of attack were used, the first to stamp out the pest and the second to kill the insects and prevent the death of the vines. Both systems were failures and two contributory causes were the fact that the pest had a complex life-history, and the Franco-Prussian war of 1870. The pest firmly established itself in the vineyards while the human quarrel proceeded on its disastrous way.

No cure could be found until the life-history had been elucidated and it is greatly to the credit of the scientific workers of those times that the story was uncovered so quickly and, in spite of the early neglect of the English work, with so much international collaboration.

The phylloxera (*P. vitifolii* Fitch or *P. vastatrix* Planchon) is an American aphid which has a different life-history according to whether it is living on an American vine (such as *Vitis labrusca*) or on the European vine (*V. vinifera*), a circumstance which much confused the issue and delayed the cure. The American vines, as is well known, give very poor, foxy-tasting wine. The European vine is the only vine giving a wine of any quality.

On the American vines the pest lives mostly on the leaves. The wingless stem-mothers suck the leaf sap and at the same time inject a substance which causes a gall to form around them. Beneath this protection they give rise to numerous living young; these leave the gall and set up house for themselves, by forming their own galls. There are no males at this time, only parthenogenetic females. A leaf may become covered with galls, or there may only be one or two present. Even so the insect causes little damage to the plant. In late summer a generation moves to the roots and starts breeding there. After a generation or two the root forms produce winged aphids, which come to the surface, and eventually lay two kinds of eggs on the leaves, small and a little larger. From the former males hatch and females from the latter. These mate and each female lays one large winter egg on the bark of the vine. The winter is passed in the egg and this hatches in spring to produce the stem-mother and start the cycle again.

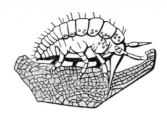

Root inhabiting form of the phylloxera, with its proboscis inserted into tissue or root of vine.

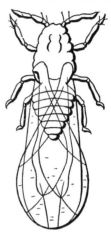

Winged Migrant Female. Hatched from the root Phylloxera, this form flies to other vines where it lays parthenogenetically, male and female eggs.

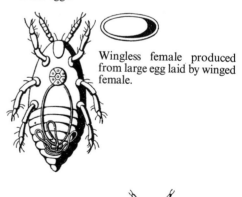

Wingless female produced from large egg laid by winged female.

Male produced from small egg laid by winged female.

Scheme of the complete life cycle of Phylloxera

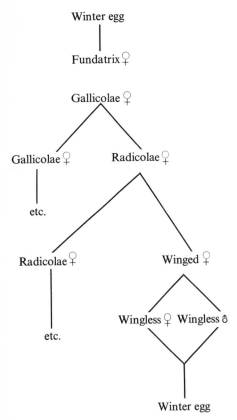

Winter egg

Fundatrix ♀

Gallicolae ♀

Gallicolae ♀   Radicolae ♀

etc.

Radicolae ♀   Winged ♀

etc.   Wingless ♀ Wingless ♂

Winter egg

The story is otherwise on the European vine. Winter eggs and stem-mothers are rare and so consequently are the leaf galls and the gall-living parthenogenetic females, though they can be found at times. The phylloxera prefers to live on the roots of the European vine. The generations follow each other rapidly in summer and a resting generation passes the winter. This is not all; the substance the phylloxera injects, which causes a gall to form on the leaf of the American vine, or a lump on an American root, is fatal for European roots. The roots swell up and quickly die when the feeding insects inject this toxin. Having killed their host, the aphids surface and seek another vine, and thus spread the infection.

The economic damage done by the phylloxera was enormous: it caused more financial harm than the Franco-Prussian war. By 1889 one and a half million hectares of vines had been destroyed out of a total of two and a half millions. France was importing wine, and vineyards that used to sell for £500 the hectare were making a bare £25 as corn lands. Wages were halved, business in the vine areas collapsed and much of the population emigrated.

The cure, 'reconstitution' with grafted vines, was a bold one. An article in the *Gardeners' Chronicle* for Dec. 25, 1880 (p. 812) outlines the insecticide treatments and the scheme of experimentation submitted by Maxime Cornu; the insecticide treatments gradually fell away as the success of the American roots was demonstrated. To 'reconstitute' the whole of the vines was an enormous task. A vineyard has some 9,000 plants to the hectare. To cover two and a half million hectares meant producing some 22,500 million plants, removing a similar number of old, dying and dead vines and replanting. By 1890 some one and a half million hectares had been done. To-day, the world over, nearly all vines are planted on resistant roots. The exceptions are the very sandy soils where the phylloxera cannot thrive and countries, such as Britain, where the pest does not exist. The moral is: never smuggle a vine back to England; you might bring the phylloxera again, a pest which could wipe out our vineries.

Wines Without Names

by Edward Hyams

Edward Hyams has cultivated his own vineyard in Kent but has now moved elsewhere. Conservative by instinct and Socialist by reason (says *Punch*), he writes in red ink for the *New Statesman* and in blue for *The Financial Times*.

The greatest of the wines we still drink have been big business for a very long time. I have in my possession an amusing account of a plea made by the wine-growers of Burgundy to a visiting Tax Commissioner in the service of Charlemagne's treasury, for remission of taxes on the grounds that their vineyards had become so crowded during the last several centuries, owing to the practice of *provignage,* (that is what gardeners call *layering*), to renew the roots, that they were no longer productive. They were, of course, putting over a fast one; I am delighted to be able to report that they succeeded, but the point here is that even in the 9th century exporting wine from Burgundy was an old trade. The same is true of the other great wine regions. But the fact remains that if the volume of wine produced by tens of thousands of small cultivators in a dozen European countries including Britain; in the U.S. and Canada; in at least four South American states; and in Australia and New Zealand, be totted up, it greatly exceeds that produced by the bigger cultivators for commerce. Wine now, as wine three thousand years ago, is predominantly a subsistence crop, not a commercial crop at all. Which is to say, of course, that in addition to the hundreds of wines known by name and reputation, there are thousands which have no name. It does not follow that there is anything wrong with them. But how do you get to taste them and find out?

Nobody enjoys a great wine more than I do and if I were rich I should drink vintage claret every day; but for many years I have been interested not only in the 'little' wines, in which a small local trade is done much as a local trade is done in farm-made ciders in Devon and Herefordshire; but in the domestic wine of the small farmer of France, of Italy, of parts of Germany and Austria and Luxembourg. The method of finding out about such wines is simple but laborious. First, it is necessary to abandon the car and take to your feet. Suitable places for such research are the Vosges, the Alpes Maritimes, the Alban and other hills about Rome, parts of Tuscany, parts of the Rhineland, the Sierra Nevada, and even the cantons of Vaud and Valais in Switzerland. It will be noticed that these, and the same is true for others I could name, are all mountain regions, and it is in fact advisable to stick to them because peasants who cultivate vines in rich plain-lands or river valleys pride themselves on the mere strength of the wine, and for quality in domestic wines you must go to a fairly high altitude. It is the poor and stony soils, the rocky hillsides, which produce wines of delicate quality. It is in such regions that I have drunk farm wines which, supposing there was enough made to justify trade in them, would have made a great name.

Quite typical was a small-holding in the Val d'Aosta from which no farmer but a north Italian could have wrung even the simple living which contents the peasant. The vineyard on that holding consisted of about quarter of an acre of hillside so steep that the farmer had to rope himself when working it: the vines were not regularly planted, for the only pockets of soil were those which had collected where an outcrop of rock held the earth from being washed down the hill. Moreover, instead of all the vines being pruned to a standard, they were each pruned according to situation; in one case, for example, the rock might provide a flat face

Edward Hyams.

on which two or three canes could be trained to get the fullest benefit of the sun in a valley so narrow that morning came late and evening early to its sides; in another case there would be a stake driven into the fissure of the rock which also held the roots, and to which the vine was trained. The vintage was a nightmare, with a man on a rope filling a basket on a rope, and showers of small boulders being sent crashing down the hillside into the stream at the bottom every time the vintager moved his feet. The wine from that quarter acre had the quality, the clarity and the lightness of a Frascati. But not, of course, every year; the great wines vary with the years but only because of the weather, for the techniques of production are exact and very carefully practised and controlled.

But the peasant makes his wine when he can find time, and he is usually in a hurry. He may be careful one year, a bit careless the next; variation therefore is not, in these nameless wines, simply a matter of the season's weather, but of the farmer's character, the health of his children, his wife's temper, the latest letter from his son doing his military service. . . . I know all about this; I have worked small vineyards, first in Kent and then in Devon, and I know very well that the difference between the best and the worst of the light white wines we make is as much due to the state of my bank-manager's temper, the progress of whatever book I have in hand, the condition of the rest of my garden and therefore the demands it is making, as upon the kind of summer we have had. If you hurry over the cleaning of a barrel, for example, what might have been good wine may very well, in a year's time, be bad vinegar.

I have, of course, drunk some shocking farm wines. I recall an experience in the Vosges where, having got into talk with a man who was tying up his vines and then set to work to help him, I was taken home for lunch and a drink. The wine we had with that meal was brown, cloudy and tasted of liquorice allsorts. It derived from a few vines of *Vitis labrusca,* not the European vine at all but a north American native, resistant to disease but with no other merits. This, by the way, is *not* a condemnation of the hybrid Euro-American vines which so

many peasants in Europe cultivate in preference to the pure European, the *'cépages nobles',* simply because the hybrids have so much resistance to diseases and pests that no special pest- or disease-control work is necessary. Many of these hybrids, with ninety per cent European sap in their veins, yield wines of the highest quality. But it remains true that there are still to be found small plantings of very old, gnarled American vines, planted in those desperate days just a hundred years ago when it seemed that no European vine could survive the phylloxera, and from which wines with extraordinary tastes are still made, nearly all of them repulsive.

It was somewhere between Genoa and Turin that I stopped one very hot day and went into a little wineshop in a village to fill a two-litre flask with local wine. This flask, of Tuscan make, is a flat glass-bottle inside a flat wicker-work case; it is kept in the car, filled with the wine of the country we are passing through. I filled the flask and then had a glass: it tasted very strongly of raspberry syrup in which a rather old tom-cat had been steeped. As an amateur of very nasty (as well as very nice) tastes, I was delighted: this was something rare and strange. After talking with the peasant-cum-shopkeeper, I was taken to the tiny vineyard in a garden right in the village. The vines were in fruit and easily recognizable as one of the *V. labrusca* varieties, the grapes being neither white nor black but red.

One thing such wine-wanderings have taught me: where the vine can be grown at all, that is where the summers are no worse than those of southern England, not one inch of soil however bad, however stony, however steep need be wasted. In France, in Germany and in Italy, not to mention Spain and Portugal, hundreds of thousands of families are kept in good, wholesome table wine throughout the year from a fraction of an acre of the roughest kind of hillside, or from some awkward corner of a field. No soil is barren to the vine, thank God, and it is worth remembering that though a single, meagerly-grown vine yields but one bottle a year, it occupies but a square yard where nothing else would grow.

Face to Face with Ronald Barton

The Bordeaux shipping firm of Barton and Guestier must be as well known to claret lovers as Earl Grey to tea drinkers. Ronald Barton retired as its Chairman at the end of 1969, after 45 years service, having joined in 1924 on coming down from Oxford. Within five years both his father and his partner Daniel Guestier had died, leaving three young men—two Guestier brothers and himself—to take charge. Now he remains on the Board as 'Consultant', and will continue his valuable visits to the trade in London for a few more years.

This interview with a WINEMINE correspondent, which took place in 1963 is re-published unchanged, Ronald Barton's further comments being inserted in italics.

WMC

There has been quite a vogue on Television at home for 'Face to Face' interviews, the object being to make the famous personality reveal the traits (preferably the bad ones) in his character. So—to be fashionable—let me start by saying that I believe you were married last summer just when all your friends were certain you were wedded solely to wine. Is this a case of bigamy or has the first wife been divorced?

RB

It is quite true that I was married this Spring, and I can assure you that it was for the first time. As a family we are long-lived and so I felt there was no hurry. My ancestor, who founded the firm of Barton & Guestier in 1725, did not die until 1780 at the age of 86 and his grandson Hugh, who bought the property of Château Langoa in 1821 and the vineyards of Léoville-Barton in 1826 died at the age of 88. So I can look forward to many years of activity and have promised my wife a silver wedding.

WMC

Is it true that after the war the outlook for claret was thought to be so gloomy that anybody could have bought say a 5me cru property for £15,000? What is the present form?

RB

It would certainly have been possible to buy a 5th Growth property for £15,000 but according to the state of the vines, buildings, etc., it might have been very cheap—or very expensive!

Owing to the great rise in price of all clarets in the last six or seven years the price of all land, in the well-known communes of Médoc especially, has risen to a fantastic extent. But these prices are inflated and I am convinced myself that recent transactions in well-known classed growths are not typical.

I was wrong here; prices of classed growth properties have continued to rise even though few transactions have taken place. Some owners I know would be willing to sell, but only at very high prices. Some owners of smaller vineyards— or rather vineyards in less fashionable districts or appellations—would be willing too, but this is only from economic necessity following two financially disastrous years.

WMC

What disturbs us is that prices go higher and higher. Is there any foreseeable end to this?

RB

There is one law which is unalterable, that of supply and demand. Prices have gone up in

Château Langoa-Barton—the family home of Ronald Barton.

recent years following short crops and increased demand. When supply exceeds demand —and we may well be approaching that moment—prices will come down. It is as simple as that.

WMC

But if world demand for fine claret goes on increasing, will it not be possible to increase output? For example, I notice driving through the Médoc that there are several miles between Margaux and St. Julien which are just uncultivated scrub. Couldn't vines be made to grow here?

RB

Yes indeed, but these uncultivated areas are the direct outcome of the laws of 'appellation controlée'. They are all outside the well-known communes, Margaux, St. Julien, Pauillac, St. Estèphe, whose 'appellation' gives a fictitious value to the wine. Disinherited districts such as Lamarque, Cussac, St. Laurent can produce excellent Bourgeois wines but will never match the quality of the classed growths, owing to the nature of the soil.

134

WMC

A year or so ago there was talk of replacing the famous Classification of 1855 by a new one. It was also said that this would cause a second French revolution. I expect you have strong views on all this.

RB

Yes, I have; not so much because I fear a revolution, but because I am in favour of leaving well alone, and I am convinced the classification of 1855 was a job extremely well done. It was not a sudden idea but the consecration of the habits and customs of years. Take for example my own two wines, the two vineyards are run as one property and Château Langoa, a 3rd growth, is always less good (though very good!) than Léoville Barton, a 2nd growth. Of course it is understandable that the protagonists of change are those who want to go up, or desire an equal classification with their neighbours.

WMC

Articles rarely say much about the species of vines planted to make claret. Members of our

Wine Mine Club, who come to Tastings as regularly as Tottenham supporters to White Hart Lane, are, I'm sure, thirsting for knowledge.

RB

There are five species of vines authorised in Médoc—Cabernet Sauvignon, Cabernet Gris (or Blanc or Franc), Merlot, Malbec and Petit Verdot. Each has its own qualities and characteristics, but the base of all good wines is Cabernet Sauvignon. Until 1940 it was always considered that a well run vineyard should contain seventy per cent to eighty per cent of Cabernet Sauvignon and the remaining twenty per cent to thirty per cent could be made up of the other four species. Some vineyards favoured one and some another and this gave each its own character. Since the war, the Merlot has come into favour because in certain years it produces more, and many vineyards now contain fifty per cent, sixty per cent and even more. I am certain myself that this tendency is detrimental to quality and, more particularly, to keeping powers.

It is now generally recognised that too many Merlots have been planted since the war. If a grower applies for authority to increase his vineyard, as opposed to normal replacement, his application is almost certain to be refused unless it is for Cabernet Sauvignon.

WMC

There is a tendency among romantically minded wine lovers to imagine that the vintage starts with exotic dancing round the maypole, with the local lovelies entrancing the eye in their traditional dress, and ends with a sort of a Mafeking night all along the line. What is the real form?

RB

In the Médoc, celebrations wait until the end of the vintage, when the pickers bring the owner the 'Bouquet', in theory the last bunch of grapes. In practice a 'bouquet' of flowers and grapes is presented but in most properties celebrations end there. I myself maintain the old tradition. The 'bouquet' is presented by a young girl who presents the hosts and their guests with a small bouquet of flowers or a button hole, and a fond embrace on both cheeks. Then we dance on the terrace but as this is before dinner, not for long! Later, strengthened by food and wine, we go on to the vintage kitchen and dance into the small hours —wildly or soberly according to taste!

The official end of vintage is the 'Ribote', which normally at Langoa takes place the Sunday after all the wine has been drawn off into cask. The property supplies a sheep, which forms the basis of the meal, bringing together everyone on the estate and the local pickers.

WMC

One other question on the vintage—I get quite a few letters from under graduates wanting to work. Are they welcome and if so, what can they expect to be paid?

RB

There is a special office in the Bureau de la Main d'Oeuvre in Bordeaux which deals with such requests and unemployment pay is stopped during picking. There is generally little difficulty about finding work and pickers will be housed, fed and paid.* But I cannot guarantee what the standard of housing and

Ronald Barton (left) studying the programme with G. R. Delaforce at the annual London tasting at which Barton and Guestier wines are shown.

feeding will be. It is always advisable, if possible, to make private arrangements, but I do know that a good number of students of all nationalities come every year, and are presumably satisfied. (* 20–25 francs 1970).

WMC

The average Englishman, huddling daily 60 ft. below ground on the Bakerloo Line has daydreams of being a country squire, patting a deer and having a friendly word with an Aberdeen Angus as he potters round the Park. Does this bear any resemblance to being proprietor of a Médoc Château?

RB

Very little, quite apart from the fact that I cannot see an Aberdeen Angus flourishing here, where only the local Frisian, accustomed to Médoc 'grass' in July and August can survive. A Médoc proprietor either pays someone to look after the place for him, which is very expensive even if the man is competent and honest, or he does it himself. I can assure

you that this is very hard work and should be a full-time job. The anxiety about the weather from early March to after the last grape is picked is constant, and there are all the worries and drawbacks of monoculture.

WMC

I'm hoping our talk will give some impression of Bordeaux life. Do you have much social life in the Médoc itself?

RB

I'm not sure that isn't a leading question put to a man who was until recently a bachelor.

No, for several reasons the Médoc is pretty quiet. In the first place most of the châteaux are not inhabited except at vintage time, and where they are, the proprietor normally looks after the place and has very little spare time. People generally don't drop in for drinks; entertainment is usually in the form of dinner. Cocktail parties have almost entirely disappeared in recent years and were always rather grand affairs.

WMC

What puzzles me is how the French can afford to dine out as they do? And indeed their capacity for getting through an eighteen franc five course menu?

RB

I remember when I was in a British O.C.T.U. we were shown, exposed on a table, the total rations of a man per day. It was staggering! I'll wager that if the normal daily fare of an average Englishman was placed beside that of an average Frenchman, the former would be the bigger pile. Most Frenchmen start the day on a cup of coffee or tea, have a good lunch and a light dinner, while the English never stop eating; snacks if you like, all day, without mentioning the greater quantity of alcohol they consume. And you must remember that the French *enjoy* their food. On a Sunday or a holiday, they will collect together and go to a restaurant for a good meal. You have seen them in a restaurant getting down to it. But you forget that this is the exception, not the rule. As regards expense, the Frenchman will economize on his clothes, the paint on the outside of his house, the cinema, racing, football, the wireless, television, etc., spending more on food, while for Englishmen the contrary is true. Remember too, that if a Frenchman appears to have a huge appetite at midday, he has very likely been away since dawn, working for hours in his garden, on his farm or *à la chasse*.

WMC

Returning again to wine, in Burgundy, due to the widening gap between supply and demand, wines are being made to reach their best in a very few years. Are you forced to do the same in the Médoc?

RB

This is a very vexed question, and nobody can really explain why 1928 made hard wines and 1929 wines which became drinkable very early. I prefer to say nothing about Burgundy, but I do not believe that Médoc wines are being 'made to reach their best in a very few years'. If Médoc wines are being drunk earlier today it is because the public like young wine—wines which their fathers would have considered barely drinkable. If wines do develop more quickly today it has little, or nothing to do with

vinification, but is due to the fact that the average age of vines is much less and the proportion of Cabernet Sauvignon is smaller. My own policy is to keep as many old vines as possible (I think I have a higher proportion of vines over 50 years of age than any of my neighbours) and to maintain the correct proportion of Cabernet Sauvignon. I am sure that in this way over the years, I make better wine, better balanced, more robust and with better staying power and I am convinced that this is really what is required. Others can make the 'pretty-pretty' wines which *can* be drunk almost as soon as they are in bottles and *must* be drunk within a few years, though I acknowledge that these latter may be a better commercial proposition . . . for the moment.

Not only is the proportion of Cabernet Sauvignon smaller, but the proportion of Merlot is considerably greater; and Merlots produce greater quantities of wine, less robust and therefore developing quicker.

WMC

By the time our discussion appears in print it will be nearing Christmas. Are we to picture you in your cellars with flickering candle deftly decanting a Magnum of 1870? What sort of image should we present of the Monsieur Le Propriétaire Château Léoville-Barton Grand Vin St. Julien at Christmas?

RB

Well, we all welcome an excuse to drink one of the treasures of our cellars in pleasant company. Lucky is the proprietor who still has a magnum of 1870, though I do not consider 1870 one of the greatest years in Bordeaux. I can hear the howls of amazement and derision at that statement and I will probably be accused of sour grapes, when I confess that it was several years ago that I opened my last bottle of 1870. It was a huge robust wine, an incredible wine, but not a typical Bordeaux, lacking the delicacy of a real Bordeaux. I would greatly prefer, if I had the choice, 1868, 1874, 1878, or even 1871, 1875, or 1877, though there is less chance of these latter still being alive. Being my first married Christmas I can assure you that I will drink an excellent old bottle: no, I almost forgot, *we* shall be drinking two.

An old vine at Châteauneuf-du-Pape, where the huge stones reflect the heat.

Rippling Kipling Rhône

by Anthony Hogg

To the inveterate Continental motorist, setting forth each year, the journey south holds something of the romance and excitement of Kipling's old trail. Though most of us would really prefer death to selling our tired souls 'for the bucking beam sea-roll of a black Bilbao tramp,' the Morris Minor 'sagging south on the Long Trail' gives the same exhilaration without the discomfort. The rivers—Marne, Saône, Rhône, Po, Arno, Tiber—wheel back like the old lost stars, the Morris grinds and heaves and there is certain to be a 'mutter overside' if the car dashes down a *Sens Interdit* when 'dear lass' is meant to be reading the map.

Of all the rivers, the Rhône is more than a landmark; it is the pilot vessel on the trail itself. For how could we reach the Riviera without road and rail following its course south of Lyon, or cross the Simplon without climbing its valley through Switzerland? As we turn south at Brigue for the Pass, it is rippling down from an icy source above Gletsch, pioneer of the route between French and German cantonments. There are no vines up here but they breed fine vintages of men from whom the Swiss Guards of The Vatican are largely recruited. Lower down in the Valais, good soil and accessibility brought the vine in Roman times or earlier, and from this point to Marseille something worth drinking—and indeed eating—is never far away.

The crisp dry white wines of Le Valais are for the most part easily recognised by name. *Fendant* is a grape; Sion, the principal town: hence *Fendant de Sion* and *Fendant du Valais*. The red wines are invariably *Dôle* and have a flinty taste. The Rhone flows out of Lac Leman into Haut-Savoie. At Seyssel, production is now concentrated on sparkling wines, few of which match sparkling white burgundy. Visitors seeking the best of the region should drink Seyssel making sure the label is qualified by *Appellation Controlée*. This excellent white wine results from soil long planted with orris-root from which essence of violet was distilled in the perfumeries at Grasse years ago. Traces of orris-root still in the soil give the wine a bouquet of sweet vi-o-lets. *Vin de Bugey* and *Roussette de Bugey* are the next best. All these are of course Rhône wines but not Côtes du Rhône, a classification limited by law to the 120-mile stretch from Vienne to Avignon.

The Grand Route N7 hereabouts has an ugly accident record but can be avoided by crossing over to N86 on the right bank. This more peaceful road, only disturbed by cement factories at intervals, soon passes the Blonde and the Brunette, the two sides of the hump of Côte Rotie. At Condrieu and at Baix there are quiet hotels right on the Rhône, well stocked with wines of Côte Rotie and Hermitage. But they are no longer cheap; neither are older vintages listed which is disappointing, for the best of these wines take a dozen years to develop fully.

Further down the road comes Tournon, bright and cheerful in summer as its twin town Tain, across the bridge, is dour. Chapoutier and Jaboulet make their Hermitage wines from the hill above in Tain, slipping over the bridge to lunch on *Quenelles de brochet*. The distinctive flavour of red Hermitage comes from the *Syrah,* the only permitted grape rarely found elsewhere. Côte Rotie must be 80

Gigondas, up and coming district near Châteauneuf-du-Pape.

per cent. *Syrah*; Châteauneuf-du-Pape around twenty-five per cent. The white wines' character is similarly governed by the *Rousanne* and *Marsanne* grapes. The best white wine of the Rhône is said to be a Château Grillet from a four-acre vineyard, which certainly cannot make more than 2,000 cases a year.

I have drunk it in Condrieu, the pleasure never quite matching the expectation. Since then I have read that a shipment was sent to Chicago where they appear to take their pleasures very seriously. Cruising, I once met a Chicago lady who was writing a project on all she saw in the Eastern Mediterranean for her psychiatrist when she got back; to make it more difficult she was writing it in French, a language she did not appear to have learnt at all. At a Chicago Banquet sixty-eight gentlemen and fifty ladies 'filled out their organoleptic report cards' on Château Grillet, while Dr Rezek, the author, embarked on an evaluation to see whether the polyethylene stoppers were the cause of the wine not tasting so good.

Châteauneuf-du-Pape, twenty minutes drive out of Avignon, is worth a visit for the view from its ruined ramparts alone. To the south, the Rhône flows on through the widening plain to its divided end; to the east the distant hills rise to the Alpes-Maritimes. Estate-bottled crus of the famous red wine often reach a strength over twenty-five degrees proof, which means an extra few shillings of duty per bottle if imported here. After drinking them from balloon glasses at La Mule, the village's Michelin starred restaurant, belonging to Pére Ansélme, a leading local firm of growers and shippers, it is hard to resist buying a few bottles on the spot.

The journey in search of wine ends at Tavel, home of the world's most famous rosé. There are different qualities, some poorer than the very drinkable rosés now made in Portugal. The best require five different grapes and a careful balance as to their proportions.

So ends the Rhône trail—
'The Lord knows what we may find, dear lass,
And the deuce knows what we may do—'
Kipling was quite right. Last time we found two speed cops cunningly concealed and were 'done' for fifty new francs on the spot.

A Professional View of Loire Wines

by John Grant

The Loire, one of the longest and most beautiful rivers in Europe, has been justly acclaimed by writers of many epochs, Ronsard, Rabelais, du Bellay and Henry James among them.

Although over six hundred miles long, its most interesting vineyards are associated with the lower half, roughly from Sancerre westward to Nantes.

My late partner, Kit Bland, a great lover of and expert on Loire wines, used to say that the finest white wines were made where the vines had to struggle for a living and certainly the latitude (47–48°) of that part of the Loire containing most of the vineyards marks the most northerly wine-growing area in Europe, apart from the Moselle (about 50°).

The Loire vineyards produce red, white, rosé and sparkling wines, but the red are of least importance. In this country the rosés are rightly popular—unsophisticated, charming, agreeable with almost any dish or when drunk as an apéritif, but to the enthusiast the variety of white wines are of greater interest.

Vinously, the Loire is the perfect lady. There is nothing gross, coarse or too alcoholic about her wines, a fault which can be found along the Rhône or in the Mediterranean vineyards. Because of their fruitiness and lack of alcohol they are nearly always best drunk young, preferably within twelve months of the vintage; I have even enjoyed bottles of Muscadet only three months old.

The vine may have been cultivated in the Loire valley before the Christian era, but the first historical reference to it is by Gregory, Bishop of Tours, in A.D. 573, who mentions the impetus given to the culture of the wine by St. Martin and his disciples, who had founded their Abbey near Tours in the fourth century. It is thought that these monks started by cultivating a black grape, which previously grew wild in the forests with which the area was at that time thickly covered. Oenological experts believe it to have been the Chenin-Noir and from it has been developed the Chenin-Blanc, the cépage most widely used in Touraine and Anjou.

Further east, in Pouilly, Sancerre, Quincy and Reuilly, the vine is the Sauvignon, precisely the same species as is used to make Château Yquem.

Near Nantes, the Muscadet gives its name to the district in which it is grown. Here one also finds the Gros Plant, which as its name suggests, is a more productive and less refined vine. Of the black cépages, the most important is the Cabernet, but the other black grapes (Groslot, Malbec, Gamay and Pinot Noir) cover a comparatively small area. The total production of red and rosé wines together is about half that of white wines.

This great wide bestraggled area has to some extent a common identity in the delicacy of its wines and the fact that they are produced near the Loire; nevertheless the growers of Muscadet have very little to say to the growers of Sancerre, by dint of the great distance which divides them.

The Loire is principally a region of small producers; for instance, the average *appellation contrôlée* vineyard makes only 324 gallons a year, an output which might be pleasing to a

The picturesque road between Angers and Tours.

'A region of small producers'.

A Muscadet scene near Château de la Galissionnière.

Guernsey cow, but does not make a living for a Loire vigneron, who has to rely on other forms of agriculture.

The Loire is not commercialised in the same way as homogenous districts like Bordeaux and Burgundy; very few of the négociants speak English or have big cellars organised to receive visitors. This is partly because their wines have in the past been consumed locally or in Paris, exporting on any scale being a new innovation little more than fifteen years old. Calling on them without prior warning or introduction is not therefore popular and people on holiday should arrange appointments through their hoteliers or through the local office of the Syndicat d'Initiative.

Many producers sell some of their wine directly to the public by taking stands at the *Concours Agricole* and *Exposition des Arts Ménagers* in Paris (shows rather like super-combinations of our Ideal Home and Food Fair Exhibitions). My firm first made contacts with many of the Loire growers by going to these exhibitions, which have played their part in introducing the now popular Muscadet as a sort of white equivalent to Beaujolais. Despite the enormous distance separating the two districts, the wines do have much in common (acidity, fruit and the need to be drunk when young).

Beginning a Loire journey near its source in the Auvergne, there are vineyards just east of Clermont-Ferrand, producing light, agreeable wines, mostly consumed locally. Their wines carry a V.D.Q.S. title (*Vins délimités de qualité supérieur*—one class below *appellation contrôlée*).

The important vineyards begin at Sancerre and Pouilly-sur-Loire. The vineyard of Sancerre is, scenically, the loveliest in the world. Les Monts Damnés at, and just after, sunset on an autumn evening, beats any romantic setting you can dream about.

Sancerre wines must be drunk young when they are high in acidity. Later they lose it, gaining alcohol and mustiness, which does not suit them. I once overheard Jean Cocteau say

Savennières with Château Roche aux Moines and the Coulée de Serrant vineyards in the background.

that he loved Sancerre better than any other white wine. Quincy is out of the way, but well worth a visit; it has no hotel nor restaurant, so do not go at lunchtime. The wine is dry, light in alcohol and marvellous with oysters. Reuilly, near-by, where I think the wines are even better, is less known and almost totally uncommercial.

At Pouilly-sur-Loire, the growers meet annually under a banner with the motto, 'Water divides us, Wine unites us', and there is indeed a unity about this part of the Loire, whose wines are not easily distinguished one from another.

Two hundred years ago the vineyards around Orléans produced large quantities of wine but its quality, to judge by the present-day wines of this area, must have been so poor that when the railway began to feed Parisian mouths with Bordeaux and Burgundy, the end came for Orléans.

Vouvray is often described as Sec, but never having met a dry one, I doubt if such exists. True Vouvray has a little flavour of honey. Sometimes it is bottled before all the sugar is turned into alcohol allowing the fermentation to continue in bottle giving the delicious *pétillant* wine, often made into a full-blown *mousseux* by the *méthode champenoise*. Montlouis across the river is a poor relation, whose wines one fears are often sold as Vouvray. Both wines and people live in little cellar houses cut into the walls of the chalky cliffs. Vouvray is a lovely village. I remember a glorious walk around it on a sunny April morning followed by a lunch of rillettes, andouillettes and bottles galore.

Jasnières and the Côteaux of the Loire are further north. A small quantity of very agreeable dry white wine is produced but little comes to this country.

I cannot mention all the Loire wines but if you ever go to see the gentle, romantic Château at Azay-le-Rideau do try the sweet wine of Aché. The growers are simple people growing apple and cherry trees all mixed up with the vines and one was greatly surprised to hear that we have apple trees and motor cars in England; but they are all charming and their sweet wines make a marvellous end to a good meal.

The only red Loire Wines of any importance come from Chinon and Bourgueil to the west of Tours. Chinon is a prettier name and a prettier place but in my view Bourgueil, although unpronounceable, is infinitely the better wine. It has a strong taste of the Cabernet grape, a little like a very heavy Médoc. It can take five or six years to reach its peak and at this point has a most agreeable aroma, suggestive of blackcurrants.

Saumur is dull as a still white wine but second only to champagne when made as *mousseux* by the *méthode champenoise*.

Anjou Rosé—from the Burgundian grape Pinot Noir—is easily the most popular Loire wine imported here; but a better wine is made with the Cabernet. Light in alcohol, large quantities of Anjou Rosé can be poured down young throats (either as a cold apéritif or with food) without serious damage.

Just west of Angers, on the north bank of the Loire, Savennières makes delicious white wine, dryish, high in alcohol and slow to mature. Very little comes to Britain, which is a pity.*

The Layon is little more than a ditch, as I discovered trying to bathe in it during the great summer of 1959. The level then did not reach my ankles but the level of Coteaux du Layon is another matter. After a few months in bottle the dry white wine is matchless as an everyday wine. I drink about three hundred bottles a year. Why the sweet type is better known I cannot imagine. Of these, Quart de Chaume is the big name but only the very old dessert wines deserve the big reputation.

This three-page journey covering six hundred miles ends at Nantes with Muscadet—dry, firm, almost unbeatable with any fish. Muscadet *must* be drunk young. Anyone who offers you a five-year-old Muscadet deserves to be coshed with the bottle. But since alcohol is disastrous in cases of concussion, a light tap with your copy of WINEMINE instead might lead to his more rapid enlightenment.

* This has now been partly corrected since Peter Dominic started shipping Coulée de Serrant, from the best vineyard in Savennières.
—Editor

Traditional wine making implements in the
Beaujolais museum at Beaujeu

Some Lesser French Wines

by Anthony Hogg

By the time you've been a student of wine for twenty years (half of them as a professional), you begin to think you know something about it. You believe that you know the names of nearly all French wines (not the individual properties, of course), and that if a trade colleague confided, for example, that he had just bought a parcel of Pomport '64 you would at least have a clue as to its locality.

That this is not the case, as far as I am concerned, has just been proved, not by some esoteric book of reference kept only by wine merchants, but by the familiar Michelin Guide of France.

In what localities would *you* expect to meet the following French wines: Vallet, Montlouis, Madiran, Lunel, Lirac, Les Riceys?

They are all shown in the Michelin Guide on the little map quite simply entitled 'Good Wines'. (The answers are also at the end of this article.)

My own results in this test remind me of an oral examination in gunnery which I endured as a midshipman in a destroyer years ago. My three months' training had been largely occupied with football, theatricals, gin, and the plotting of 'enemy' positions during fleet exercises. My knowledge of gunnery would not have filled a 6-out measure.

The exam, conducted by a young lieutenant, took place at 14.00 and began with several glasses of port calculated to put the candidate (and the examiner) at ease. Although the young lieutenant handsomely doubled my 18 marks out of 100, 36 per cent hardly commended my diligence to a keen gunnery commander when I returned to my parent ship.

The Michelin map made me delve deeper, remembering that wherever a gastronomic star is awarded, both the specialities and the wines of the place are mentioned. A cursory look through the A's revealed the following wines: Arbois and Puppilin—at Arbois in the Jura. Irouléguy and Jurançon—at Ascain in the Basque country. Fonsalette, Côtes de Ventrous and Gigondas—Avignon.

I soon concluded that 'Lesser Wines' still forms quite a field for discovery, even though many of them have been imported in recent years.

At the Cro-Magnon at Les Eyzies in the Dordogne (whose trade must have been hit, incidentally, by the closing of the Lascaux caves) they commend Prayssac and Saussignac, while at Les Glycines, the other hotel, the wines are Pomport and Panisseau.

All these are local *ordinaires*. The best red wines of the Dordogne come from the communes of Creysse, St Sauveur, and Bergerac, being entitled to the name Pécharmant. Better known and available in Britain is the white, sweet, and luscious Monbazillac—a change from plain Sauternes or St. Croix du Mont. Cahors, where the red improves considerably with bottle age, stems from vineyards on the Lot farther south. Château Bonnecoste, another Dordogne property, was well known to the late Warner Allen, who once described in WINEMINE a day's truffle hunting with the owner.

149

Pau. Local wine, Madiran; local sight, the Château.

Among lesser wines now available here from the south-west corner of France are Jurançon Sec, Blanc de Blancs and Gaillac Blanc or Rouge. The Gaillac district near Albi did quite an export trade in the Middle Ages.

I must have first met Jurançon and the other popular Basque wine, Irouléguy, as a schoolboy in 1924, when my father took the family for the August holiday to the inn at Itxassou, fifteen miles inland from Bayonne. Permanently inhabiting this pub was an Englishman named Feuerheerd (a well-known name among port shippers in those days). With his wife and daughter, he kept dogs, which we soon decided had been hastily evacuated from our bedrooms. Their fleas laughed at all our efforts with insecticides in those pre-D.D.T. days.

'The fleas that tease in the high Pyrenees', remain a painful memory. After a week we had to evacuate to Bayonne, where my mother, offering prayers in the Cathedral for delivery from pestilence, was incensed to be bitten yet again!

From the Spanish border to Marseille there is an abundance of sweet white wines from Banyuls to Muscat de Frontignan. There are, too, countless reds in the Languedoc, of which Château Roubaud, Costières du Gard is as good as any. This is one of many lesser wines shipped here by Asher Storey & Co.

More highly rated, but neglected both by shippers and wine writers, is the sparkling Blanquette de Limoux—described as 'So golden and light, so natural and gently sparkling that one is never tired of watching it bubble and drinking it afterwards'. Limoux is near Carcassone. The russet Mauzac wine bears golden grapes, the name Blanquette relating to the white silky down covering the underpart of its leaves.

As far back as 1349 the Lord Lieutenant of the Languedoc decreed that only Mauzac wine should be made at Limoux and in the sixteenth century the local Abbots of Saint Hilaire were busy extending the vineyards. Later, like Dom Perignon in Champagne, their successors discovered—probably after leaving the new wine in a closed pitcher one April—that it had become sparkling. Today, Blanquette de

Just France!

Limoux is a *méthode champenoise* wine with an appellation of origin, and not more than twenty-two gallons may be made from each three hundredweight of grapes.

A more curious sparkling wine is that of Les Riceys, which has the legal right to call itself 'Champagne'. Once I made a detour to these two little villages, east of Chablis, bringing home a bottle from the local shop, where I thought it would be cheap. The price was over 40s.—a matter of keeping up with the Heidsiecks I suppose. Rosé de Riceys also has its own appellation; if your curiosity is excited, I suggest a bottle at Riceys' flowered restaurant, whose speciality, an amorous écrevisse, might excite it even more.

The delightful whites and rosés of Provence give much pleasure there, but deprived of their supporters—Mediterranean sun, sea, and sea food—may be disappointing elsewhere. Perhaps, too, there is the psychological element —how can a bottle have the same appeal with a herring at Skegness as with *fruits de mer* on the Côte d'Azur?

Some years ago I hoped to buy some of Monsieur Bodin's Cassis rosé, which he makes at Mas Calendal, his home on the hill above the port. I can certainly recommend a visit to any enthusiastic gardener; Monsieur Bodin has collected rare plants from all over the globe. His Japanese garden, in particular, remains a memory. But—and this is the trouble with Provence wines—the lovely rosé cost too much to be a success in England.

With surcharge on top of duty and import tax now added, wine-drinkers may welcome any suggestions as to how to save a shilling or two per bottle without noticeable detriment to their drinking.

More prominent here than it was five years ago is a red wine called Gigondas which is described in *Wines and Vineyards of France* as 'Whole, well rounded-off, robust, reminding the drinker of Châteauneuf-du-Pape'. As the crow flies, only ten miles separate the two, so the association is not surprising.

Among other 'little knowns', I always enjoy two dry white wines of Savoie when stopping near Chambery *en route* to Italy. Each bears a V.D.Q.S. appellation and their

In the Pays Basque.

names are Aprémont and Jacquerre.

In Chatillon in the Jura there is an inn called Chez Yvonne, quite isolated, with the river Ain rolling by the garden gate. This is where I would go to drink the wines of Arbois —red, rosés, and white, the *vin jaune* and the *vin de paille*.

Asher Storey import no less than eight, but they cannot import Yvonne's *Truite de l'Ain,* nor her *Morilles à la crème* to go with them. Still less, the cook, Yvonne herself. She is twenty stone and worth her weight in gold, so the import duty would make an even more fascinating calculation than those we already endure!

ANSWERS TO QUESTIONS

Vallet	the best district of Muscadet, Brittany.
Montlouis	The district of Touraine opposite Vouvray.
Madiran	Red wine met around Pau.
Lunel	A Muscat wine of the Hérault départment.
Lirac	A.C. wines red, white, and rosé of Côtes du Rhône.

Sunday morning in a Champagne village.

La Champagne

by Pierre D'Harcourt

La Champagne is the country; Le Champagne the wine and I have always thought La Champagne a much undervalued province. Except for visiting the cellars, no one, I suppose, would dream of spending a holiday there. Nor, since the Bureau du Tourisme seems to hold the same misguided view, would I encourage them to at present, for accommodation is rare, expensive, and badly placed.

Yet Champagne as a region is beautiful and various, a fact difficult to realise if one takes the big national road via Chalons to the south. Following the well sign-posted 'Circuit de Champagne', however, along quiet country lanes, one finds a hilly country of graceful vineyards, many of them famous, and of ever changing and often dramatic views, such as the one from Hautvillers down to the valley of the Marne. The route also takes one past some fine twelfth- and thirteenth-century churches.

I would like to dwell for a moment on these churches, and on antiquities generally, for it is extraordinary, in a land so fought over, so destroyed, that so much is still left standing. There are Sacy and Les Ormes, primitive and fortified, the church of Villedomange and the miraculous and enigmatic virgin in the chapel above the village, Coulommes, Avenay—to mention only a few in the 'Côtes des noirs' north of the Marne. And taking names haphazard in the 'Côtes des blancs' to the south—Cuis, Flavigny, Le Mesnil-sur-Oger, with, at the southern apex, the walled city of Vertus, tiny, proud, and isolated, encircled by its rampart promenades, with its arched gateways and many charming old houses to be discovered in unexpected corners. Reims herself is a very cradle of French history, possessing, besides the Cathedral in which nearly every French king was crowned, a blackened Roman Arc de Triomphe, one of the few existing in the north of Europe. Epernay, rival to Reims in the wine trade, with her incomparable air of nineteenth-century prosperity, bears witness to the wars with her very *lack* of antiquities.

I think that it is this sense of history and of wars, of fields soaked with blood, combined with the pride and stimulation of producing one of the world's great wines, that give Champagne and the Champenois their especial character.

The Champenois is both industrious and fatalistic. He lives in a country made gay and rich by its vines, and by his own endeavour, yet time after time he has watched the fruit of these endeavours brutally destroyed. Driving through this rolling country, sparkling with its particular dancing light, and coming suddenly upon a thousand quiet crosses, neat and tended in a garden hedged with box, one cannot but be struck by the tragic. It is these reminders, these memories, which help to make the people dour and deep.

The Champenois, also, is a man of the north; which is perhaps why vintage time here is celebrated with somewhat more restraint than people expect. Yet it has its own traditions. It is the culminating moment of the year, the time to which we have all (for here, nearly everyone's life is in some way touched by wine) looked forward as to a supreme test, a goal, an end. Indeed, in wine-growing countries the New Year starts psychologically with the ending of the vintage. The Church too participates, Mass is said very early, and the sermon deals most practically with the problems of the vintage, reminding us particularly of our traditions of hospitality towards our visitors.

During harvest time no man's day is his own, everything else comes to a full stop. Out of the question to have your drains cleared, your roof mended, all are in the vineyards picking, helping in the *vendangoir*, or in the kitchen of

155

Looking towards Verzenay across the Champagne countryside.

those who take in *vendangeurs*.

These vendangeurs are mostly people from the mines in the north of France, the same groups of families who have come year after year. They are tough people, used to hard work —and indeed grape-picking, sometimes under a boiling sun, sometimes, as has happened, in a freezing mist, up at dawn, home at dusk, can be exhausting—but this is their holiday, fresh air, old friends to be met again, good pay. Their presence is vital to us and they are always given a warm welcome. Families of gypsies form part of the backbone of the pickers, and they too are excellent workers. But it is essential to arrange that they stay in their own groups, or fights develop.

The vintage gets under way slowly, different areas starting at different times. But as the days go on the sense of excitement mounts, and one sees more and more little groups, waist-deep in vines, the bagnolets or sunbonnets that many of the Champenoises still wear, spotting the green like huge white bindweed flowers.

In the evening, towards the end of the vintage, one sees the last lorries, carts and tractors (for everything on wheels is mobilised) returning with the workers, bunches of grapes hung behind their ears, faintly tipsy and triumphantly fatigued. On the last night there is a party, called the *cochelet,* to which in the big champagne houses, it is the custom for the heads of the firm to come. Special dances are connected with this party, one of which is performed around a carpet, rather in the fashion of a Scottish sword dance.

When all is over, Autumn seems suddenly to set in, and I associate these shortening days with the unforgettable heady smell of the heaps of crushed skins from the presses deposited for manure at the edge of the fields.

Shooting can now start in earnest. There are pheasants, partridge, pigeons, hares, some birds of passage, and quite a sufficiency of wild boar; for a short time the activity of the vintage is replaced by the activity of the sportsmen—every Sunday a-bustle with gun-filled cars. Then the mist comes down in earnest and Champagne settles down into her long hard winter when the lovely dazzling painter's light becomes at best but a glare.

157

PALAIS IDEAL

by Anthony Hogg

Wine, they say, is good in moderation. That's why in the first Summer WINEMINE (1963) it was given a miss for a page or two to tell one of the world's strangest stories. But first, you must imagine yourself postman of a small village, forty miles south of Lyon a hundred years ago before the days of cars or bicycles, doing a daily round of twenty miles on foot.

One night you dream you have built a strange palace of stones—a weird, grotesque fairy-tale palace, a pot-pourri of architectural styles you have never even set eyes on. You awake, but there is no forgetting the dream; every detail has followed you into consciousness. The urge to build is irresistible. But you have no materials, no tools and no training.

This was what happened to the Postman, Ferdinand Cheval, at Hautrives around 1864 when he was 28. It was ten years before the dream began to fade from memory. And then, one day on his round, he tripped over a stone and picked it up. The touch of this flat stone, shaped by the weather of centuries, was enough to revive his great ambition. 'Nature has been the sculptress', he said, 'I will be the architect and mason'.

Thenceforward he returned from his rounds laden with stones and began to build his Palais Idéal. On his round he would make piles of these stones, returning at dusk or setting out before dawn to collect them. It was a labour of Hercules lasting 26 years, resulting in a masterpiece which will always fascinate the *cognescente* of the visual arts and must evoke admiration even from those whose creative endeavours go no further than snowmen and sandcastles.

The dimensions—26 × 14 × 26 × 10 metres —and the illustrations give some idea of the postman's feat, but a visit is needed to be charmed by the sculpted animals—elephants, bears, crocodiles and ostriches—such as one could only meet in a dream.

The Palais Idéal was building from 1879 to 1912. Ferdinand Cheval was then 77. Still he worked on, building the family tomb in the cemetery, where he was finally laid in 1924. Perhaps he has another little niche in history not far away from Lear and Lewis Carroll.

If you happen to be one of those volunteer postmen delivering parcels at Christmas, take comfort when the burden becomes intolerable —from Postman Cheval, whose bag was *never* empty.

TRAVEL NOTE: Turning east in Vienne, a secondary road runs parallel to N7 to Hautrives through Beaurepaire d'Isère. The journey south can continue through Crest and Nyons, those bound for the Mediterranean rejoining N7 at Cavaillon, east of Avignon. This route passes through the Drôme lavender fields—an ocean of blue in June—and is not particularly hilly.

Palais Idéal. The western Facade.

Palais Idéal, a grotesque, wonderland world.

The Wine When It's Red

by Arthur Eperon
'not quite cultured' travel correspondent
who describes some adventures in Eastern Europe

The man from Minsk weaved his way to my pavement table carrying two glasses and a bottle of Russian champagne-type.

'Roll on the boat!' he shouted. 'Praise the Lord and pass the Guards' Division.'

He leaned perilously and aimed the champagne at the glasses. Swaying, he hosed some over my head, some in my lap and a little in each glass.

'Bottoms up!' he shouted and emptied his glass.

Vera, my eye-shadowed blonde interpreter from Leningrad University, spoke petulantly to him in Russian. He pinched her bottom.

'Send him away, Mr. Eperon,' she said. 'He is not cultured.'

To be 'not cultured' in Russia is a very serious social black.

'He's a splendid chap,' I said.

My friend returned with another bottle. 'I'm a splendid chap,' he said. 'Guards' Div. They free me from the Germans. They make me their mascot.'

He sprayed more champagne about. His aim had improved with practice.

'Roll on the bloody boat,' he repeated.

Vera was nearly in tears.

'He is giving you the wrong impression of our people.'

The manager arrived. He was black-coated, suave and sorry that I was being molested.

I was not being molested, I said. I was happy to be drinking with such a friendly citizen.

The manager said he understood. But this was an *International* hotel. Perhaps if my friend and I went across to the railway buffet.

'Picture a troopship just leaving Bombay,' my friend began.

Vera was nearly hysterical.

Then an understanding sort of copper arrived. My friend agreed to go with him on one condition—I gave him my tie as a souvenir.

'Will he go to prison?' I asked Vera.

'I'm afraid not. He will be treated and sent home.'

I was glad. I didn't want a man wearing my old school tie to be in Minsk prison.

As we left, we saw him and the policeman in the station buffet drinking beer. My friend was singing lustily in English: 'Officers don't bother me, I've seen 'em all before. Bloody tight trousers with stripes down the side, bloody great pockets with nothing inside . . .'

'Splendid chap,' I said.

'Mr. Eperon,' said Vera, 'sometimes *you* are not quite cultured.'

East Europe, like West, has its teetotallers, drinkers, topers and drunks. Russia tended to have more than its quota of drunks until recently. Beer is sold in street stalls, vodka is very cheap and housing is still difficult. A whole family in one room, all shouting or listening to the radio, and Mum, No. 18 on the list for the kitchen shared by twenty families, promotes pub crawling among Dads. Pubs in Russia are romantically called 'Beer Points'. You can start at 'Beer Point 1' for a quick one on the way home and you are at 'Beer Point 7' or 'Champagne Point 2' before you remember that you were supposed to be baby-sitting.

Unfortunately, though vodka is cheap the better wines are dear. They cost about 18/- a bottle in Moscow. The best place to drink them in Moscow is the boat-café on the Moskava river opposite the huge Ukraine Hotel.

If your Russian is dodgy, just take a label off a bottle and use it as a pub visiting card. Georgian wines are way out in front, Southern Russian wines are mostly brothers to Australian or Spanish sauternes and the local pink champagne tastes like fizzy lemonade laced with pink gin.

I nominate as No. 1 a wine called Georgian No. 1. Judging by results, it is slightly fortified. Goorjuani (Georgian No. 3) is drier. The red Georgian, Mukazani No. 4, has a high reputation, but a real red-lover like myself would rate it about Valpolicella Standard.

Don't count on choosing your wine outside the big cities. Distribution is uncertain. If you hear a rumour of wine, go, whether it is Caucasian Riesling or Moldavian Aligote. It will soon be gone.

Hungary and Rumania take their wines most seriously. Hungarian wines are well known here. Bull's Blood of Eger is solid and lovable, Tokay—still made from bursting, over-ripe berries—is luscious, too dear and too sweet. Rieslings from the South West (Balaton), on the Yugoslav border, are good but too sweet. So are Rumanian Rieslings. Rumania's vineyards are by the Black Sea, suffering rough winters and sudden summer heat, so all the wines tend to have a lot of sugar. The best wines are the Cabernets, which compare well with French wines from this grape but have a sweetness out of character.

Near Mamaia, the Rimini-like beach resort of the Black Sea, are two huge experimental vineyards where five hundred wines are made from imported grapes. Luli, my Rumanian interpreter, claims that I once tasted fifty of them in one day. That was in an old cellar. Last time I went there, she made me drink at the newer, scientific experimental station outside a sort of aircraft hanger. She says I managed to 'taste' twelve half bottles in two hours and finish with a full bottle of Cabernet.

Rumanian wines such as the Tirnave Perla and Riesling cost 12/- in a Rumanian hotel and are worth it, mind you. At the Lido in Bucharest, you dine on very good food indeed, around a swimming-pool with artificial waves which are liable to land a bikini-girl in your lap. At the gypsy cafés, where the Rumanians eat goulash and the whole family drinks as they did in France before industrialism raised its nasty head, you can get a potent ordinaire for sixpence a half pint. Rumanians collect their wines in a jug from off-licences, which keep the barrels on the pavements outside the window. They also drink a slivovica called Tuica. The with-it drink, called Amalfi, is a pony glass half full of local red vermouth and half Tuica, with ice and lemon. It is very effective.

Rumanians are Latins surrounded by Slavs and they think and drink Latin. Bulgarians are Slavs who drink Slav in a professional but rather sad way. They make many wines along the Danube—mediocre but not bad. Here in Britain you can buy their Gamza red or Grozden riesling for about 12s. a bottle.

The Czechs make wine—in the Bohemian valley of the Elbe, where they have made it since 1248, and in Slovakia. I suggest you drink Jugoslav or Rumanian—the excellent food deserves something fairly palatable—and make the most of the good Pilsen beer and even better slivovica.

In Poland, you drink beer and vodka. You certainly drink. Drinking is the national hobby.

The Poles are an independent people. I was drinking quite recently in the old town of Warsaw with an ex-RAF man and some factory workers when they noticed that two plain-clothes policemen had followed me into the pub.

'I shall kill them now,' announced a huge worker, wielding a beer bottle.

'Wait until we get them into an alley,' said the airman.

'I've a better idea—let's get them drunk,' I said.

The Poles thought this was splendid.

They grabbed the unfortunate coppers.

'You will drink with our English friend,' they announced.

Frightened at first, the policemen started to drink. Then they warmed to their new found task. When we left, they were still toasting me. Duty is duty in Poland.

Romantic Rhineland

by Peter Heyworth

Peter Heyworth, music critic of The Observer, describes his recreation in Who's Who as 'wine and escape'. As this article shows his register embraces Fuder and Fugue with equal ease.

To anyone who has ever sat enthralled through Wagner's 'Ring' a glimpse of the Rhine brings a special tremor of excitement. Whether it is the modest stream that makes its way through the gentle, hilly country between Basle and Zurich, the majestic canyon that it has carved between Koblenz and Bingen (this is the romantic Rhine beloved of tourist brochures) or the vast, flat expanses of its delta as it finally reaches the sea near Rotterdam, the sight of the river out of which Wagner's great epic arises and to which it finally returns (for the universe he created is in 'Götterdämmerung' engulfed in fire and the water of the Rhine) stirs a great hoard of associations.

Wagner was only one of the countless German romantics, poets and writers as well as musicians, for whom the Rhine had a special meaning. 'Der heilige deutsche Strom' became a great emblem of the reborn German nationalism that grew out of the Napoleonic wars, (and it is perhaps worth adding that, in spite of what has since happened, the German nationalism of that day was little different from the Italian *risorgimento* of Mazzini and Garibaldi whose virtues English liberals still extol). Few rivers are richer in historical and cultural memories.

Alas, this romantic aura does not of itself guarantee beauty and fine wine. Only in the fifty odd miles between Koblenz and Bingen does the scenery have the dramatic quality that we like to associate with the Rhine. And as for the vine, although it grows almost all the way from the Swiss frontier in the south to the suburbs of Bonn in the north, the part that produces the wines that are famous in Britain under the generic term (unknown in Germany) of hock, is surprisingly small.

I don't by any means wish to imply that these lesser-known wines are of no interest. On the contrary, there is the Kaiserstuhl, a small mountain that sits in freakish isolation in the middle of the broad river valley between the Black Forest and the French Vosges, whose volcanic origin gives its wines a very distinctive quality. And, only recently a miserably thin, modern opera was redeemed by a most delicious Neuweier Mauerwein Spätlese that comes from the country north of Baden-Baden. It was so fresh, robust and admirably balanced that I brought a bottle home, where it refuted the nonsense that none of the lesser Rhine wines travel.

There is also that far too little known and drunk tributary of the Rhine, the Nahe. Because its character mixes a little of the Moselle with that of the Rheingau, it is perhaps less immediately distinctive than either, and hence less written and talked about. But this brings the advantage of lower prices, and the best value in ordinary German table wine that I have come across in recent years was a Schloss Böckelheimer 1960.

But, of course, the three regions, the areas where some of the greatest white wines of the world are grown (I cannot hide my belief that the greatest of all come from the Moselle) are the Rhinegau (Rheingau), Rhine-Hesse (Rheinhessen) and Rhine-Palatinate (Rheinpfalz). Now the trouble from the point of view of the would-be visitor is that none of them is set in the famous and most picturesque part of the river, although the Rheingau is nearest to it. But in fact this is something of a blessing, for anyone who imagines that the 'romantic' part of the Rhine is still, in the mid-twentieth century, a good place for a quiet

Die Pfalz, a conspicuous Rhine landmark approaching the Rheingau.

Klusserath, Moselle.

A Moselle vineyard pattern.

Assmannhausen, where that rarity a German red wine is made.

The Chapel of Holy Laurentius, opposite Leiwen, Moselle.

'The rather grand hotel Krone at Assmannhausen'.

'Take the cable railway'

Leiwen, Moselle.

Hotel Jagdschloss Niederwald.

bibulous holiday is in for a shock. This part of the river is not merely a centre of communications of first importance, but is to the huge urban masses of the Ruhr what Southend and Brighton are to London.

As a result, there are mainline railways and main roads on *both* banks, while the river itself is as alive with barges as the London docks, not to mention an unending procession of pleasure steamers. No wonder the poor Rhine salmon now generally tastes of dirty oil. Unless you are peculiarly gregarious, this part of the Rhine is not for week-ends. What you are likely to find in an average hotel tends to be disappointing.

There is one exception that I know of: the rather grand Hotel Krone at Assmannhausen, on whose terrace you can (for a price) sip some splendid wines while looking on a part of the most magnificent stretch of the river. (It is worth while taking the opportunity of drinking one of the few red, and, I think, the only fizzy red wine grown in Germany, even if the experience is curious rather than remarkable.) But to my mind it is preferable to take a cable-railway up to the Hotel Jagdschloss Niederwald, where in the quiet (week-days only) of the surrounding hills you can enjoy what on my last visit was an impressive list of the Rheingau.

But the visitor to Germany must prepare himself for one disappointment, and for me it is a serious one. The pleasure of drinking young, modest, light white wines in their actual place of origin is intense: they have a freshness and a charm which never quite survives travel. But as soon as one decides to have a bit of a bust and starts to look around for something that is both grand and reasonably old, one is speedily made aware that such bottles are few and far between. For this the German economic recovery is largely to blame. Because it is expensive, wine in Germany is a prestige drink, and the higher the price, the higher the prestige. As a result, a German business man would not offer an important customer anything less that an Auslese with his fish. An exaggeration? Maybe; but the fact remains that in Germany (as in France) great wines are drunk long before they are at their

169

Deidesheim, Palatinate.

Sundial (Sonnenuhr) near Urzig, Moselle.

170

A much improved road follows the Moselle from Trier.

A striking vineyard pattern across the Rhine at Lorch.

Bernkastel, Moselle.

Choice of hotels at Bernkastel.

best. The really top Rhine wines almost always have a very prominent sweetness in youth that makes them repellent to my palate until they are at any rate five years old or so. Then—and only then—do they acquire that full, resplendent balance that makes them at their best such superb after-dinner drinking. In 1957 I remember finding a Schloss Johannisberger Beerenauslese 1949 still far too sweet (the immense sugar content had not yet been fully consumed by the acid). But I fear that should I return today with enough ready cash, I should discover that it had long ago disappeared down the gullet of some magnate from Dusseldorf. Perhaps there is, after all, something to be said for his counterpart in Birmingham, who firmly believes that Liebraumlich is tops. At least he does not take ambrosia out of *my* mouth.

No, the sad truth is that if you want to sample fine German wine of some age, you are more likely to find it at the (few) English merchants who know something about this rather specialised field. And here let me add that any wine merchant who omits the name of the grower from his estate-bottled hocks, either doesn't know or doesn't care, and should be shunned like the plague.

So far I seem only to have warned of the perils rather than of the pleasures that confront the wine tourist on the Rhine. But the villages of the Palatinate such as Forst and Deidesheim, nestling in a great ocean of vineyards, are enchanting; and of all German wines it is these, strong in taste yet comparatively restrained in nose, that make the best companion to food. There is a good variety of them on the list of the Kanne in Deidesheim, a restaurant that is backed by the famous Bueklin-Wolf estate. For me, however, the joys of tranquil scenery and wine are best enjoyed on the Moselle.

LEISURELY CHARM

Of the thousands of tourists who make their way up the Rhine, only a handful turn half-right at Coblenz, and, leaving the majestic stream of Germany's greatest river, pursue the gentler Moselle as it winds its way south-west to Trier and over the frontier into Luxembourg and France.

The change is immediate. If the Moselle lacks the sheer grandeur of the Rhine it preserves a quiet, leisurely charm that roads and railways, barges and pleasure steamers have long taken away from its big sister. There is quite a bit of tourism in the most picturesque and romantic stretch of the river immediately upstream from Coblenz. Here the scenery is rather like a miniature Rhine, with castles and dramatic hills tumbling precipitously into the water. But this is not where the best wine is grown. That begins only in Erden, and it is in the twenty-odd miles between here and Trittenheim that there lie the tiny villages whose names are renowned wherever the qualities of great Moselle are recognized. Here the landscape is less dramatic than lower down the river, and, although the terraced hills still tumble down to the water, the country has a more gentle, rolling ease. Perhaps it is in part an association of ideas, but for me the great line of hills that stretches downstream from Bernkastel is one of those views that never fails to make my heart leap, as I survey the vineyards of Graach, Wehlen and Zeltingen shimmering under a hot August sun and reflect on pleasures to come.

For anyone with a taste for wine and the simple joys of life, there are a score of tiny pubs in this area that can provide a base for a cheap holiday. For those who attach more importance to creature comforts it would be better to stay in the Drei König Hotel in Bernkastel, the county town (as it were) of the Mittelmosel. Of course some of the unhurried, bucolic charm of the villages is lacking, but in compensation there is the awe-inspiring wine list of the Hotel zur Post (also nice to stay in, if you can get a room).

But drink leads to food, and to the tricky question of when to drink your Moselle. Of course if you live there, you drink it at all times and with all dishes, and I must say that no wine benefits more than a fresh, young Moselle from being drunk at its place of origin. But it is essentially a delicate wine, whose quality lies in fragrance rather than in staying power. In England I see no point in drinking it with spicy

Trier, centre of the Moselle wine trade.

The Saar at Wiltengen.

or heavily sauced food, which it simply cannot stand up to. If what you want is a sound, knock-about white table wine, then for heaven's sake turn your eyes towards the Palatinate, and paradoxically in an off-year, which can provide this sort of thing better—and far cheaper—than the Moselle.

No, Moselle is a wine for special occasions, when you don't mind spending a little more for the very distinct qualities it offers. At table I would only consider it for light fish dishes or perhaps an absolutely straight-forward Natur Schnitzel, and even in this field it has formidable competitors in Burgundy as well as the Rhine. Where to my mind it has no competitors is as a summer apéritif, sipped in the garden before lunch or dinner with a dry, unsweetened biscuit. Then its unique qualities blossom, its wonderful blend of lightness and fragrance, the remarkable subtlety of its nose, the refreshing, prickly *Spritzigkeit* that soon goes if you don't drink it young. No produce of the earth seems so complete an embodiment of spring as this supremely elegant and refulgent wine. But it's no good expecting pleasures like this for the price of an odd Beaujolais. The very nature of the Moselle, its slatey soil, the hard winters and late summers that give the wine qualities unattainable in easier climates, also make it hard and costly to grow. Even in Germany, cheap Moselle is only too often a nasty, sugared drink. So don't expect too much for under a pound a bottle, and on the whole stick to estate bottlings. One pound for an apéritif, you say? Well, think of the price of four large gins and tonic—and aspirins for afterwards. In contrast to gin, Moselle induces a gentle euphoria and sense of well-being that no alcoholic concoction can rival.

But the Germans keep their finest wines for after dinner—and rightly so. It is at this stage of the evening that the *Auslesen* come into their own. Because they are made from selected grapes they are fuller, sweeter and rather more powerful than their untitled cousins. But whereas the Rhine *Auslesen* can easily become rather too much of a good thing, too full, too perfumed, too resplendent, like an overdressed dowager, Moselles never lose their inimitable sense of style. The acidity that is never absent from these wines, and which makes them so poor in an off-year, in a good year tempers the sweetness and holds it in balance. The result at its best is a wine that transcends mere sweetness and dryness. In the *Beerenauslese* class their price can go up to £5 and beyond; and the awful thing is that they can be worth every penny, for these are the greatest white wines grown on this imperfect globe—Château d'Yquem being as nothing compared to the almost unbelievable sensations of taste and smell that emerge from a really great and mature wine from the estate of, say, J. J. Pruem of Wehlen. And their staying powers are something that one does not usually associate with wines from this region. For instance J. J. Pruem's 1949 Wehlener Sonnenuhr feine Auslese is still superb, while his feinste Auslese of the same year only recently reached its peak.

KARL MARX'S OLD SCHOOL

Trier is itself the centre of the Moselle wine trade. It is an enchanting city with Roman remains that has now recovered from extensive war damage, and it makes an agreeable centre for a wine holiday. The town itself is the head-quarters of some of the finest estates, many of which are still in the possession of the cathedral, the provincial seminary, and Karl Marx's old school—the Friedrich Wilhelm Gymnasium. And it is near Trier that the two tributaries of the Moselle join their mother. The Ruwer and Saar wines are generally grouped under the heading of Moselle, but in fact they both have distinct characters of their own. A useful description of the Ruwer's distinguishing marks eludes me, but the Saar has a highly individual astringency. In a poor year its wines are sour and nasty and are largely used to make Sparkling Moselle (I served Schloss Saarfels once and no one noticed that it was not champagne. In fact it lacks the *brio* of good champagne, but it is a far pleasanter drink than some of the acidulous cheap champagne that is too often provided at receptions). In a great year like 1959, however, the Saar comes into its own with wines whose fragrance, dash and delicacy almost outdo even the Mittelmosel itself.

175

FRANCONIA

by William Wake

Kenner trinken Frankenwein
Erhalten Herz und Nieren rein.

Franken wine for the connoisseur
—Keep the heart and kidneys pure!

References to *Franconia* have the same emotive quality as those to *Samarkand;* the words sound to English ears with the same peculiar mixture of familiarity and strangeness. Franconia is in northern Bavaria and stretches from Spessart forest, east of Aschaffenburg across Würzburg to the Steigerwald and farther to Frankish Switzerland lying between Bamberg and the Bayreuth of Wagnerian fame. Frankish or Franken wine is grown between the Steigerwald and Bamberg but mainly around Würzburg, the capital of German Baroque, heavily damaged on the night of March 16th, 1945, but now substantially, though not completely, restored.

The central building of Würzburg is undoubtedly the Residence, built by Balthasar Neumann for the Prince-Bishop. This building, with a superb ceiling by Tiepolo to its entrance staircase, a ceiling fortunately preserved, is well known to students of the Baroque but its architectural importance to this journal lies in its vaulted cavern-like cellars, which form the main cellarage for wines from State-owned vineyards.

It was my good fortune to extend a tour of the Residence to its cellars under the guidance of the Kellermeister. Under the north wing of the Residence lie some 300 casks of various sizes, but mostly of 7,000 litres (1,540 gallons)

maturing the good Franken wine. Made only of oak, these casks have a useful life of about 70 years (a symbolic period?) and those made for special occasions have elaborate hand-carved end pieces. The story goes that wine of the 1540 vintage was found in such perfect condition in 1684 that a special cask was made to contain it. The cask was built to honour the wine and was hence elaborately carved. On account of the date it is known as the *Schweden-fass,* reminding us of the military exploits of the thirty-years war. This must have been a wine, or were the earlier Würzburgers more credulous than we? When it was finally finished, perhaps on one of those occasions when the whole cellar is used for a celebration and lit by candles stuck in Bocksbeutel, or arranged across the reinforcing timbers at the circular end of the 50,000 litre (11,000 gallon) cask built in 1784 and flanked by two 25,000 oval casks, which are retained for historical and sentimental reasons as they have not held wine during this century.

STEINWEIN

Wine in the familiar Bocksbeutel is often referred to as *Steinwein*. However, Steinwein is that prepared from grapes grown on the steep southern slopes of the *Steinberg* which overlooks the railway station at Würzburg. It

177

The pictures on this and page 176 are of The Residenz, Würzburg.

is divided into separate vineyard holdings and among the more important are those owned by the Bavarian State and by the older charitable foundations—and what more charitable foundation could our ancestors lay down than a first-class vineyard? Progress appears as a fine broad concrete road (verboten to tourists; it is a working road only) across the slopes of the Steinberg. The different holdings on the hill are separated by concreted walls as if jealously on guard, the ownership being indicated by some device or motif. Only a small proportion of Franken wine can, therefore, be Steinwein although the Bocksbeutel is used for all Franken wines. Other very superior sites exist on the Main before it reaches Würzburg and some by lesser tributaries of this great river. *Iphofen,* for example, is a village name known to all lovers of Franken wine and it was there on the wall of a small inn that we found the advertising rhyme which heads this report.

We sampled among other wines in the Residence cellar, straight from the top of the cask by a syphon, two Würzburger Stein wines, one from a Riesling and the other from a Scheureben grape, both 1963 and both more promising than the average of 1963. They will stay two or three years more in the cask according to the judgment of the Kellermeister. About 75 per cent of the Würzburg State wines are bottled in Bocksbeutel, which bin flat more satisfactorily than one might imagine. Much of it comes to England where Messrs. S.F. & O. Hallgarten are well-known importers. The remaining 25 per cent goes into ordinary bottles for use in Weinstuben where wine is usually served by the glass or in small glazed earthenware jugs of quarter-litre capacity all inscribed 'Trinkt wie eure Vater aus Stein den

WEINSTUBE

We have now come to the important subject of drinking wine in Weinstuben. There is no exact equivalent of these cafés where wine rather than tea is taken, with or without food, though coffee can be ordered and would be willingly served. In Würzburg there are two very famous foundations, the *Juliusspital,* a foundation of the Prince-Bishop Julius Echter

in 1576, and the *Bürgerspital zum Heiligen Geist* a foundation of a patrician family, von Steren, in 1319. Both still function as homes for old people, the former as a hospital in the modern sense; both were badly damaged in 1945 but have been restored; both possess famous vineyards on the Steinberg and elsewhere in the region; both have their own Weinstuben. The *Bürgerspital* has reconstructed the eighteenth century atmosphere of its Weinstube with a multitude of small rooms, including one in a cask with just room for four persons and a table. How warm and comfortable it must be in winter? The Bürgerspital also supplies those *Spital-Blatz,* circles of baked, wafer-thin, flaky pastry about six inches in diameter made for nibbling when drinking Franken wine.

THE BOCKSBEUTEL

High above Würzburg, on the opposite bank of the Main, stands the mediaeval fortress of Marienberg. Its steep slopes are faced with vines. The fortress itself houses the *Main-Franconian Museum* with its artistic treasures, the greatest being the *Til Riemenschneider* carvings (1483–1531). The last room in a tour of the Museum contains the history, in relics, of Franken wine. Presses, casks, glasses, and—the history of the *Bocksbeutel.* The Urform was a spherical container of glazed earthenware, but, as the Kellermeister told us, this was inconvenient for the pocket. Something rather flatter better fits the poachers' pocket (Bocksbeutel), so the present form slowly appeared during the late eighteenth and early nineteenth century and has altered little since 1900.

One last important question we put to the Kellermeister: 'How does one become a Kellermeister in Würzburg?' One is apprenticed to the State winery for a number of years and finishes with two semesters followed by practical examination at the State educational establishment for Horticulture and Wine, which is a few miles away at Veitshöchheim.

There are two good reasons for making Würzburg a holiday centre. Baroque architecture and Franken wine. Perhaps you know know nothing of the former; ignorance of both is surely inexcusable.

* Drink wine as your father did, out of a stone vessel'.

Hungarian Rhapsody

by John Levett

The main vintage celebrations had just ended when I made my jaunt around Hungary's vineyards. Perhaps it was just as well. Otherwise, Magyar hospitality being what it is, I might never have found my way across the border again. As things were, it was difficult enough. Hungarian cellar-masters do not distinguish between 'tasting' and 'drinking', and most have a wine-bibbing capacity—while remaining steadily on their feet—which would put a French peasant to shame. Even the youngest—certainly the prettiest—cellar-master I encountered, a twenty-two-year-old blue-eyed blonde in the Balatonfured state cellars, would have found no difficulty in putting Nikita Khrushchev well and truly under the table.

The first word I heard in Budapest was Egésegeré (say it egg-ay-sheg-er-ay), the Hungarian equivalent for 'Bottoms Up!' It was still ringing in my ears as I boarded the train for Vienna. It is not for nothing that one of the oldest greetings in the Hungarian language translates as 'Wine, Wheat, Peace'—with wine always first!

It was not, in fact, at a vineyard, that my wine-tasting marathon began. Hungary's present annual wine output runs at about 125 million gallons, and a great proportion of that finds its way into the Budafok state cellars, a thirty-minute car ride from the centre of Budapest. And it was there that I started.

Budafok is really a suburb of Budapest built on wine cellars. In all, about fifteen miles of them honeycomb the limestone hills, and one cellar I saw had storage capacity for nearly five million gallons of wine. Here, all Hungary's export wines come to mature, and a great quantity of wine in cask goes to hotels and restaurants in Budapest and the provinces.

Though the cellars themselves may resemble the catacombs of Paris, there is nothing archaic about the Budafok bottling system. I saw a Czech bottling line with an hourly throughput of 2,400 bottles, and two Chelle lines from France with a combined throughput of five thousand bottles an hour.

Work there was a serious business—and so was the tasting. I ran the whole gamut of Hungary's wines in an hour, starting with a light, dry Móri Ezerjó (literally: thousand times good of Mor) and concluding with a superb, five-puttonyos golden Tokay Aszu.

Most of the wine stored at Budafok, however, comes from the hills around Lake Balaton, the 'inland sea' which the Hungarians use as their holiday playground.

Most important of the Balaton wine districts is that encompassing Badacsony, Balatonfured, and Csopak, an area of about ten-thousand acres with the hill of Badacsony in the centre. Volcanic soil and favourable climate combine to produce distinctive Rieslings. But a different vine produces what I regard as the most distinctive of the Balaton wines—the light, bright Keknyelu (Blue-stalk).

When I had tasted (and swallowed) a long line of Rieslings, Keknyelus, Furmints, and Muskotalys (yes, muscatel), my pretty blonde cellar-master brought me her speciality—a delicate and delicious Pinot Gris, grown and bottled by the Hungarians as Szurkebarat (Grey Friar). It was certainly good. But how she managed to provide me with a long lecture on Hungarian viti-culture as we drank—she had matched me glass for glass—I never discovered.

Fertod Castle, near the Sopron vineyards. Haydn was the *Kapelmeister* here for many years.

The State wine buyers complain that far too many varieties of vine are grown in the Badacsony-Balatonfured-Csopak district, and they could be right. The vinicultural institute, situated on a slope of Badacsony hill, made a thorough survey a few years ago discovering at least seventeen varieties under cultivation.

Variety has its advantages, of course, but it does not lend itself to the production of a really great wine. The peasant's reluctance not to keep all his eggs in one basket should eventually be overcome—or at least, the number of vine varieties grown will be reduced to a manageable half-dozen.

A long drive north of Lake Balaton is the ancient town of Eger, one of the first towns to be settled by the migrating Magyar tribes when they came here more than a thousand years ago. High in the town is the old castle, with its grisly cell full of skulls and bones—the remains of a company of two-hundred men who died defending the town from the Turks in 1552.

Today the town is famous for its 'Bull's Blood'—a name which legend has it was bequeathed by another army of Turkish invaders. With a garrison of two thousand men, so the story goes, Captain Istvan Dobo held off a besieging army of 150,000 Turks. But a Turkish soldier on a 'recce' spotted some of the Magyar defenders swilling down pots of the purple wine of the region—and reported back to his O.C. that the Hungarians were drinking bull's blood to give them strength. 'So the Turks scarpered.'

The wine, of course, has nothing to do with bulls or blood, and in fact, I was told by the director of the State cellars at Eger, very little of it is drunk there today. It is made from the juice of three varieties of black grape—70 per cent Kadarka, 15 to 20 per cent Burgundy and 10 to 15 per cent Médoc Noir. It is the most full-bodied of full-bodied wines, with a bouquet all of its own.

Not all the vintage goes to the production of Bull's Blood. I tasted a good 'Médoc', a full red 'Burgundy', and a good quality Cabernet as I walked around the cellars. And I enjoyed the wine most drunk in the Eger valley—a delicate, white wine called by the poetic Magyars, *Leanyka,* or *Little Girl.*

An interesting feature of the town—apart from the castle and the fascinating Turkish minaret—is Arnyekszala Street. One side of the street is lined with doors leading into cellars cut into the hillside—for like Budafok, Eger is honeycombed with underground passages and cellars.

At the Balaton cellars I had been struck by the youthfulness of the cellar-masters, most of them in their twenties. At Eger there was more maturity, an air of greater dignity, more fitting to the type of wines produced. And in the famous Tokay cellars, fifty-five miles east of Eger, I found the kind of solemn atmosphere one associates with vintage port.

183

Not that I was offered any the less to 'taste'—but each drink was accompanied with such a wealth of oenological information that I felt myself getting hiccups as my mind and my throat both tried to swallow at the same time. Never mind. Only a hooligan would swill Tokay like draught bitter, and the learned cellar-master was only trying to get me into the right frame of mind.

Though four wines—Aszu, dry and sweet Szamorodni, and Furmint—are grown on the sloping Tokay hills, it is Tokay Aszu which has built Hungary's reputation as a wine-growing country.

Like Sauternes and the Rhineland dessert wines, Tokay Aszu depends upon the 'noble rot'—the shrivelling and partial rotting of grapes as the result of attack by *botrytis cinerea*. The sugar content of the grapes increases to as much as 60 per cent, compared to the 20 per cent or so of grapes which ripen healthily in the sun.

The shrivelled grapes are hand-picked and pulped into a sticky paste—though without crushing the pips. This paste is then added by standard measures—the puttony—to each 30 gallon barrel of most of that year's vintage. Depending upon the number of puttonys of paste added to the barrel is the description '3-puttonyos', '4-puttonyos', or '5-puttonyos' which appears on the Tokay label. Only occasionally is it possible to produce a '6-puttonyos' wine.

The Gonc keg, as the 30-gallon Tokay barrel is called, is never completely filled, allowing for a certain amount of oxidation and the growth of a special Tokay 'flor' on the surface of the wine. Maturing can take up to eight years, but is usually completed in something over four.

Szamorodni, is made by crushing normal and shrivelled grapes together, without selection. In a good year when there is a high proportion of shrivelled grapes, a sweet Szamorodni will be produced. In other years, the result is a fine dry wine. Dry Szamorodni makes a fine aperitif. 'Forty drops before the soup', say the Hungarians, and they should know. They cool it to about 46° F.

Sweet Szamorodni, on the other hand, is a dessert wine, though even this should be slightly chilled. 'But Aszu,' said a younger, but still earnest, cellar-master, 'must be drunk at exactly the right temperature—12° Centigrade.' On my Farenheit thermometer that works out at 54°—sufficiently cool to interest the palate, but warm enough to release the superb bouquet.

Back in Budapest, with the cloudy memory of many local wines reluctantly sampled on the way, and a travelling bag full of assorted gift bottles, I called at the big Unicum distillery where dozens of different liqueurs and spirits are made.

Top of the list is the superb, but fiery, Barack Palinka, distilled from fermented apricots; once your throat gets acclimatised, any other fruit brandy is outclassed.

Before touring the distillery on tottery feet, I sat in the big, comfortable office of the director, Mr. Gustav Eleman, sampling one after another of his products.

As we talked, a man in a white coat came in, opened a sideboard in the corner and took out a small bottle. I goggled. There was no doubt about it. It was a miniature Johnny Walker.

Mr. Eleman saw my face and smiled. 'It is for comparison,' he said gently. 'You see, we produce our own Scotch whiskies—but to make sure that the flavour and the bouquet are just right, we compare them with the products of your own bonny Scotland.'

I know the thrusting nature of these Hungarians, and I knew that their wine and spirit industry had just embarked on a big export drive. I had a momentary vision of mass unemployment on Speyside. But one thing puzzled me—I had seen little barley growing on my trips around Hungary.

'Where do you get your raw materials for your whisky?' I asked, trying to keep the concern from my voice.

'Please,' said Mr. Eleman with a shrug of his shoulders, 'we have lots and lots of grape spirit—what else should we use?'

'Egésegeré!' said Mr. Eleman.

'Egésegeré!' I replied as I tipped my glass.

Sljivovica!
In Peace and War

by Ian Ramsay

On a spring Sunday morning, driving out of Belgrade into the rolling green hills of Serbia, there is sure to be a wedding procession on the road. A column of gaily decorated farm carts, rattles along the *pavé,* the horses as excited and lively as the drivers, the passengers shouting and singing, hats and streamers waving to all. Only the bride herself, on the most richly ornamented cart, sits demurely, with eyes downcast and a solemn apprehensive mien, as custom demands. Somewhere in the column, a band of swarthy, unshaven, dark clothed Serbian gypsy musicians will be making loud, wild and exhilarating music: Serbian 'kolas', and folk songs predominating, punctuated with ferocious drumming and shrill blasts on a trumpet. The column moves along at a hard gallop.

Apart from the bridal couple, the significant elements in the procession are the music and the bottles of Serbian plum-brandy *sljivovica*. Bottles will be brandished at cars, or waved by young men at any girl they pass. Gestures from every cart invite the overtaking motorist to halt and drink with them. The entire procession will hold up the journey to ply you with drink, and if you drive past without stopping, you may be sprayed with jets of *sljivovica* as you go.

This is all done in the most friendly and uninhibited way, typical of the gay Serbian— and indeed all the Jugoslav people. It was not always thus.

In the dark days of 1944 when I was a British Liaison Officer with Brigadier Fitzroy McLean's mission to the Partizans, there was no *sljivovica* for ordinary consumption. Civil war and the German occupiers had spoiled the

lovely blue plum orchards. Trees had been cut down for firewood, as a reprisal, or as part of a scorched earth policy. Few men had time to tend their orchards, or to distil their health-giving *sljivo* in iron tubs in back gardens.

In the Montenegrin mountains, where I was attached to the Second Partizan Corps, some 20,000 strong, *sljivo* is traditionally a staple of peacetime life. It is given to quieten children hardly able to walk, it is swilled to cure toothache, and used as a cure for colds and fever, rather like the Highlander's dram of malt whisky.

After the war, when I was Military Attaché at the British Embassy in Belgrade, my chauffeur, Djordje, a typical young Serbian, would bind his head with a *sljivovica*-soaked rag if he had a headache. As a cure, he preferred hot wine impregnated with red peppers,

187

On the road from Ljubljana to Ormoz. Picture on previous page is of vineyard and church at Jerusalem.

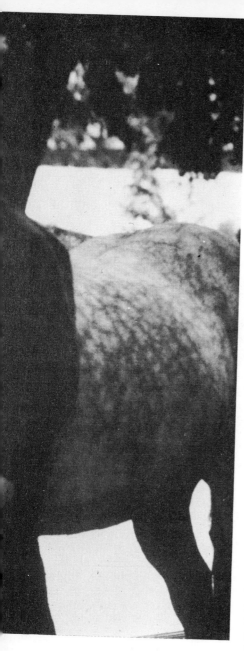

lemon, and *sljivovica* to the modern medicaments we tried to press on him. And his own remedies were certainly effective.

In the Partizan Hospitals of 1944—often ruined huts in the mountains or forests—*sljivo* was at times the only real medical aid available. The terrible ordeal of amputation without anaesthetics was perhaps slightly eased by the heady spirit before the operation. Often, too, *sljivo* had to serve as a rough antiseptic for wounds, or to help convalescents from typhus to endure the long marches, usually by night and in single file, often in snow or mountain rain. But the Partizan army as a whole was—to anyone who knows the Jugoslav in normal times—a surprisingly abstemious one. (Its wartime morality was ferociously puritan, too.)

During the months in the mountains, I hardly ever saw any alcohol available for social consumption and I can only recall one single day when the American, Soviet, and British Liaison Officers attached to our Headquarters were each given a small glass of rough *sljivovica* by the Jugoslav Corps Commander. This was to celebrate the capture of the Montenegrin town of Niksic that morning.

To return to happier post-war days, what an important wine growing country Yugoslavia has become! More and more wines and spirits are being exported and there are more to come. Among those already here but insufficiently recognised, is the dry *Žilavka,* a golden green wine produced in the sun scorched vineyards of the Mostar area—inland from Dubrovnik. This is a strong wine, from a mountainous arid countryside of sharp, scattered limestone with wild aromatic flowers and herbs growing among oak scrub. Another wine, which so far, I have hardly seen outside its native area is *Kavardaci,* a heavier red wine from Southern Macedonia, not far from the Greek border, where the summers are hot and long.

Slovenia, the nearest of Jugoslavia's six Republics to Austria, is a beautiful land of forest, steep-sided mountains, blue rivers full of trout, and the best known and largest vineyards in Jugoslavia. The areas round the towns of Ljutomer, Radgona and Murska Sobota, in

Staircase leading to the Ormoz Winery—six storeys under a hill.

Riverside motel near Belgrade.

North East Slovenia, close to the trisection of the Jugoslav, Austrian and Hungarian frontiers, produce most of the Jugoslav wines now so well known in the United Kingdom. An excellent, if rather sweeter white wine from Slovenia, which so far is not I think available here, is *Ritoznojcan,* the politest translation of which is 'The sweat from Rita's back'.

The Dalmatian Isles produce a large number of wines of varying quality and colour, a few rather acid and inky, but some very rewarding. Many of the best come from tiny arid and rock strewn vineyards built on terraced cliffsides. Among those one can find more easily is *Grk* (Greek), a yellow brown wine from the lovely isle of Korcula and the vineyards around Dubrovnik. Grk is a grape variety, the grapes when half dried making the very sweet *Prosek,* a dark dessert wine, whose

high strength drawing higher duty might make it difficult to establish in this country.

Bosnia, being traditionally a Moslem area, produces few wines even today, but towards the north east in Serbia there are some good ones. The *Fruska Gorski Biser* (Pearl of the Fruska Gora Hills), is too sweet for some, but has an effervescent quality which appeals to others. The Danube banks, downstream from Belgrade, are famous for their fruits: melons, peaches, strawberries, cherries, plums (and of course *sljivovica*); and not least for its rich sweet grapes from vineyards nurtured by rich earth and high rainfall. *Smederevka* is one of the wines from this countryside, which is well worth drinking. Further south and east, *Prokupac* is the most pleasing. It comes from the Nis-Prokuplje area, 120 miles south of Belgrade.

191

The Maestro at work.

Working at the Wine Museum

by Cyril Ray

Somebody once told me—I think it was Walter Sichel—that there were no fewer than 52,000 different German wines. I haven't much of a head or a memory for figures—I can't even remember the number of my car or of my passport—but this particular one has always stuck in my mind, for it occurred to me at once that this meant you could drink a different German wine every week of your life if you lived to be a thousand—and what a good way it would be of passing the time. (Whereas a thousand a week for a year wasn't really practicable, I sadly concluded.)

There is no such handily memorable figure for Italian wines. One Italian author recently published an enormous book on the subject, in the index to which 703 different Italian wines were listed, and was promptly taken to task by another author, who claimed to have noticed several serious omissions, though his own book listed no more than five hundred or so.

I haven't even got round to counting how many Italian wines there really are—for one thing, it depends a good deal on how you count them. For instance, one of the commonest grapes in Piedmont, the most important wine-growing province in Italy, is the Dolcetto which, in spite of its sweet-sounding name, makes a dry red wine. According to where it is grown, it is called Dolcetto; Dolcetto d'Alba; Dolcetto delle Langhe; and Dolcetto d'Ovada; and they all taste much of a muchness to me—I have never been able to tell one from the other. Is this one wine, or four? The Blauburgunder of the German-speaking Alto Adige is the Pinot Nero of the Trentino, immediately next door: one wine or two?

There is the Chianti Classico, the Chianti Colli Aretini, the Chianti dei Colli Empolesi, the Chianti dei Colline d'Elsa, the Chianti Colli Fiorentini, the Chianti Colline Pisane, the Chianti Colli Sénesi, the Chianti Montalbano, and the Chianti Rufina—one wine or nine? To say nothing of the Chiantis of the various big firms that are usually sold under their house names—Ricasoli, Frescobaldi, Ruffino, and the rest of them.

But however you tot them up, there is only one place in Italy where you can taste—not all the wines of the country, I admit, but a reasonably wide selection of them, and that is the Enoteca Italica Permanente, or Permanent Italian Wine Museum, which is housed in the old Medici fortress of Siena. Because the great difficulty in the way of studying Italian wines in Italy is the enormous insularity of each province. For just as the Florentines, who eat gigantic beefsteaks weighing a couple of pounds apiece, can't imagine how the Venetians keep body and soul together on fish; the Bolognese think the Romans barbarous in their addiction to baby lamb; and the *ravioli* of one

place is the *agnolotti* of another; so it is with their wines. The Sassella of Lombardy, for instance, is a very good red wine indeed, by any standards, and is made of the same grape as the similarly fine Barbaresco of Piedmont, the province next door. But you are very unlikely to find a Sassella in a Turin restaurant, or a Barbaresco in Pavia, only a hundred miles away, for one city is in Piedmont and the other is in Lombardy.

So it was with a deep sigh of relief, when I was trying to finish my book on Italian wines,* and realised that I still had to taste quite a few that I hadn't yet come across, and refresh my memory of those I hadn't tasted for years, that I discovered that there, in the enchanting hilltop town of Siena, picturesquely cellared in the old dungeons of the Medici fortress, were at any rate wines bearing no fewer than 385 different labels. I put it that way because they are not precisely *all* different wines—some are different growers' versions of Chianti, say, or Valpolicella—but quite enough different wines from all over the country to fill most of the gaps in my knowledge and experience. For there is certainly nowhere else in Italy that I

know of where I can lean on the counter, as I have been doing day after day for weeks during the past winter, calling now for a glass of Tocai Friulano, say, from almost on the Yugoslav frontier, and now for a Nuragus from Sardinia, chasing a Grumello from a couple of thousand feet above sea level, within sight of the Austrian Alps, with a sweet, sparkling red Aglianico del Vulture, grown on the slopes of an extinct volcano right down in the very instep of Italy, from a grape the name of which (Aglianico=Ellenico) is a reminder that this was once a part of Magna Graecia.

Not that wine-tasting is all fun, whatever the envious may think. I find that I can taste only a few in a day, for my taste-buds and my sense of smell soon become jaded. And not all Italian wines are as easy to take as clarets, say, or hocks. There are sweetish red sparklers—in fact, I have just mentioned one of them—which you have to be very much in the mood for, or else they taste like Wincarnis and Eno's. They still *look* like that, even when you *are* in the mood, and the very look can be off-putting. Yet they have their place in the scheme of things. They are quite natural phenomena,

194

and they can go very well with a summer picnic. The red Lambrusco of the country around Bologna is just such a wine, though dry rather than sweet—lots of froth as it is poured out, which soon subsides into more of a prickle than a bubble, and very well that prickle goes with the rich foods of Bologna, which is to Italy what Lyons is to France: the belly of the country, the gourmet's paradise, cradle of great cooks, and the envy of cities less sybaritic.

Anyone can visit the Enoteca: it is open seven days a week, from ten in the morning till midnight, for wine by the glass at the bar (at fifty lire a glass for most of them: sevenpence ha'penny or so), or to buy bottles to take away. The restaurant, where I have lunched and dined has been closed; in its place—I am sorry to say—there is now a night club.

I don't seriously recommend my own programme, of trying to taste every wine they have, in a matter of weeks, making notes on every one of them, unless you want to be put off wine for quite a long time. There were sunny Siena days, I must admit—for the sun sometimes shines in Italy in November—

when I came out of the cool of the Enoteca with the taste of a rich, sweet Moscato still clinging to my teeth, and a Lambrusco bubble or two still in my belly, and cast wistful eyes at the open-air beer kiosk that someone has rather saucily set up at the Enoteca's very entrance.

But I always managed to resist temptation: luncheon was awaiting me around the corner, and under my arm was a light fresh young Bardolino, bought at the Enoteca bar, and I can't think of a prettier wine for a lightish luncheon. And there was an old Barolo waiting to be decanted for my dinner, and that's a serious wine indeed, as I think even a Frenchman would admit. And it was thanks to Enoteca that I could be here in Tuscany, with a Venetian wine to look forward to for one meal, and a Piedmontese for the next, which is something of a feat in Italy.

© Cyril Ray.

* Cyril Ray finished it successfully: The Wines of Italy *(McGraw Hill, London, 4 gns)* was awarded the Bologna prize in 1968 and became the accepted work on the subject.

—*Editor*

195

Author and grandson

Wine Farmer in Tuscany

by Vernon Bartlett

I once opened a supplement to *The Times* on 'Some Wines of Europe' with an enthusiasm that may be excused in the producer of some of them. Not many of them, it is true—a mere 560 gallons—but the three views I most enjoy on our little Tuscan farm are, one, the view from my study of the forest-covered Pisan hills; two, the view of the towers of Lucca down in the valley; three, the view of our casks in the wine *cantina,* with their contents chalked on them in Giuseppe's painstaking writing. I cannot claim to be a pioneer, like Edward Hyams growing his vines in Devon, but few experiences in a fairly varied life have given me more satisfaction than that of sitting at the great stone table outside our villa, and drinking wine that I have helped to make.

The supplement gave me a shock. I could not complain that five and a half pages of it were devoted to the wines of France, for I would rather drink them than any others—except, possibly and occasionally, a slightly-chilled Mosel on the terrace of a *Weinstube* overlooking the river that gives the wines their name. But Italy makes more wine even than France, and I should have expected that more space would be devoted to them than a mere quarter page, beneath half a page devoted to the wines of Spain.

NO CO-OP

I suppose the fault is ours—and when I write 'ours' I do so not as an Englishman but as a wine-grower in Italy. A wine-grower on a small scale, as are nearly all the wine-growers in our neighbourhood. Our wine is entitled to be called *Chianti dei Colli Pisani*—Chianti from the Pisan hills—but none of it reaches your wine merchant or your favourite little Soho restaurant. We have no co-operative society to buy our produce, as they have in roughly equivalent areas in France. My market is the local bar at the bottom of my drive or the cottage inhabited by some farm worker who wants to buy a demijohn of something that isn't faked. It is drunk, in other words, by people who are much less interested in a wine which, as far as possible, repeats the same qualities year by year, and therefore merits a label and a date on the bottle, than in one which accurately reflects the climate of the particular year in which the grapes were grown. He expects the wine to contain a little sulphur—and often it contains far too much—but he greatly distrusts the advice of the expert who would do this or that to correct the defects of nature. And the result is that, with relatively few exceptions, the foreign visitor cannot depend upon the label on the bottle, even if there is one.

After my first *vendemmia,* I persuaded a doctor of agriculture from the *Consorzio Agrario* to visit our wine *cantina.* Giuseppe, the *contadino* who makes our wine, was pleased and flattered until this expert arrived in a dark suit and a white collar. Thereafter it was useless for the doctor to advise the addition of potassium metabisulphite, tartaric acid or any other chemical with the help of which a wine can be made which will resemble itself year

197

The author and Giuseppe.

after year. I did, in fact, insist that we should follow the doctor's advice; the result was that we produced some of the best wine in the district but were unable to sell it at a profit, partly because the large-scale dealers in town can bring in cheaper, mass-produced wines from the south, but mainly because the rumour went round the local bar that our wine had been doctored. I was left with a dozen demijohns of wine that I could not sell because I had spent some money on having it improved —a result which pleases our palates and our guests, but which decreases the possibility that my small farm will ever show a profit.

198

TROUBLES IN A WET SUMMER

The second *vendemmia* followed a disastrously rainy summer which gave us a wine with an alcoholic content of only 9 per cent, as against 11 or 12 per cent the year before, and some treatment was obviously advisable. But Giuseppe, who has made many thousands of gallons of wine in his time, was against it, and who was I to argue against him? It would, he claimed, be a waste of money to add an expensive wine of higher alcoholic content. We should sell it all, admittedly at a very low price, to local farm workers as soon as it was ready to be drunk. Remembering how much mould and mildew had attacked the grapes, despite four or five sprayings with copper sulphate and sulphur, I had to admit that he might be correct in his estimate that not much can be done to improve the wine; remembering all the dismal articles in the newspapers about the poor quality of the year's wine, I suspect that he will find every other producer trying to sell the stuff as soon as it is ready to be drunk.

When the *vendemmia* began, I insisted on the rejection of all affected grapes, and I discovered that there are few more unpleasant activities than separating the brown, squishy bad grapes from the good ones. Scores of affected bunches were thrown away, but scores also went into the crusher when I was not looking. We had little outside help for the picking, and, by the second day, we were all less careful. By the third and last day, so many beastly-looking grapes went into the collecting baskets that, for a time, I doubted whether I should ever again want to drink our wine. That doubt has since disappeared; I consider that a meal without its glass of wine is only half a meal, and I have no doubt that our wine is still purer than any wine we might buy locally.

PADRONE BUFFONE

Then there was the affair of the white wine. Very little of it is made in our district, and what little is made goes through much the same process as the red wine—it consists of white grapes which are passed through the crusher and then left to ferment in the vat with their skins, pips and stalks. Very occasionally the wine is made *alla Francese*—in the French way. The covering of skins, pips and stalks is removed as soon as the grapes have passed through the crusher, and the 'must' is allowed to ferment at leisure. But the risks attaching to this slower fermentation make it very unpopular; our neighbours come in and stare at the cask containing our first effort to make wine in the French way, as though it might at any moment explode. But I have at least achieved one great victory; I have convinced Giuseppe that by adopting the French method, a white wine can be made with black grapes, a very good wine into the bargain.

METHODE CHAMPENOISE

This, at first, he flatly refused to believe. He is a great admirer of champagne, which he has never tasted, and the spare corners in the *cantina* are filled with bottles which he hopes will turn into a sparkling wine of the Asti Spumante type. The corks are not wired; they are tied down only with strong cord, but he assures me that the *padrone* on one of his previous farms made 'champagne' in that way. He is enough of a nationalist to doubt whether most French wines are as good as most Italian wines, and he suspects that some skulduggery is the cause of the much higher prices paid for the wines of France. But he admits that French champagne (for he insists that the name covers all sparkling wines) is superior to the Italian varieties. And when I produced an Italian book in which he read out, painstakingly, word by word, the statement that the main component of French champagne is a black grape, then and then only would he agree to crush black grapes for our white wine *alla Francese*. And one of my few triumphs in the *cantina* was when I found him holding up against the electric light a glass full of juice from our black grapes—it was, he had to admit, as pale in colour as any white wine he had ever made.

Most of the contributors to WINEMINE and many of its readers are experts. It must be very clear that I am not. Had I been, I doubt if I should have bought myself a small-scale farm and vineyard in Italy at a time when the workers upon whom agriculture depends are trekking as fast as they can from the farms to the factories. But I have few regrets; if I were not spending money on the effort to keep these few acres in production, I should be spending it on some much less useful hobby. And we have no reason to be ashamed of our wine. Perhaps Giuseppe, with his long experience, and I, with my wider access to information about wine culture in other countries, will be able in time to turn out a wine of which we can be positively proud. And at moments when my wine encourages a pleasant optimism, I think to myself that perhaps, sometime in the future, *The Times* supplements will find it worthwhile to devote a whole page to the wines of Italy.

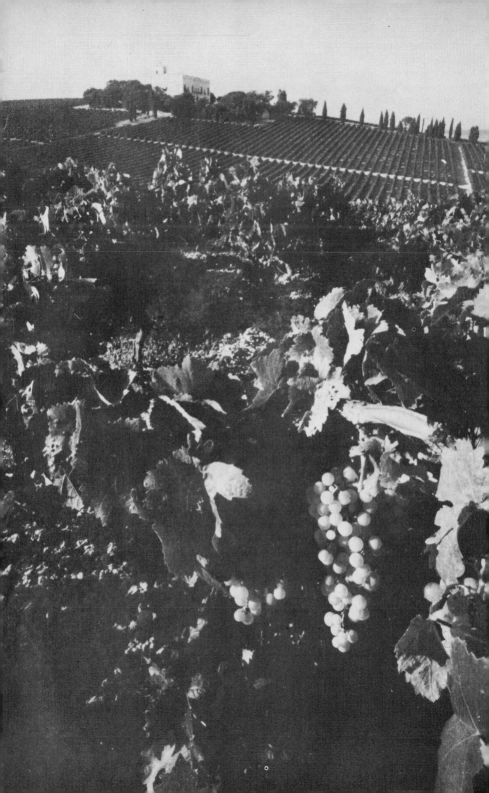

La Vida de Jerez

Fiesta in Jerez! It could be almost any time: the great Easter fair, for instance, or the procession of Corpus Christi, when the Calle Larga is covered with evergreen branches; or it could be any of a thousand private fiestas, with flamenco music in the patio, and gallons of excellent wine. But throughout the Christian world one feast must stand supreme: Christmas. And throughout the wine countries there is another: the feast of the vintage.

Christmas is quite unlike other feasts. Spaniards love to live in the street and to celebrate their fiestas in public, but not Christmas. It is a family party, to be enjoyed at home. Christmas trees are rare and are regarded suspiciously as pagan importations, while Father Christmas is an even more recent innovation that is apt to be mistaken for one of the obscurer aspects of American aid. The houses are decorated with nativity scenes, beautiful with their coloured lights, shepherds and Wise Men riding on horseback. Before Christmas small boys spend weeks making smaller, but finely constructed, nativities, which they take round the streets, collecting pesetas from the passers-by—a rather more pious version of our 'penny for the guy'!

The climax of the Jerezano's celebration comes on Christmas Eve and in the early hours of Christmas morning. After hearing Midnight Mass the family gathers round the *brazero*—a hopelessly inefficient, singularly uncomfortable, but rather picturesque heating appliance. Then there is a glass of oloroso, and the carols begin. Although the words are highly suitable, the tunes are frankly moorish in origin, and the singers are accompanied by the *zambomba*—a small drum covered with rabbit's skin, into the centre of which is stuck a piece of cane. The hand rubs up and down this stick, rebounding off the drum to produce the sort of noise that a rhythmical window cleaner might make with his wash-leather.

All this ceremony happens in the modern, sophisticated town of Jerez; but it also happens in the biblical simplicity of the austere, white Andalusian hill villages. There, when one is hearing the harsh voices and moorish music, or looking across the bare room through the curtainless windows into the glimmering cold sky, one knows Christmas as it was in Palestine two thousand years ago.

On New Year's Eve, when the clock strikes midnight, on each stroke everyone in the house must pop a grape into his mouth and eat it: difficult in the time allowed, but delicious! Each grape represents a month, and they are preserved for the feast, hanging on rafters in the peasants' houses. The story is told of how Queen Isabella II came to Jerez long after the vintage and asked to see every stage in the making of sherry. It was a royal wish and not lightly to be ignored, so grapes such as these were bought off the peasants and a whole butt of excellent wine was produced.

The greatest spurt of energy comes on Twelfth Night: the day of the Three Kings when presents are given. No one goes to work, and it is devoted entirely to the children. But as they are impatient creatures the great fiesta moves back a few hours to the evening of the eleventh night, when there are great parades through the streets and the Three Kings give presents to the excited multitude.

Yes, when one says 'La Vida de Jerez' one might just as well say 'La Fiesta'. For despite the wine, and the sun, and the friendliness of the people; despite the beauty of the old town and the rolling landscape of vineyards between Jerez and the sea, it is the fiestas that stand out most clearly in the memory. And the most elaborate of these is the *fiesta de la Vendimia*—the vintage feast.

The vintage starts in Jerez roughly on

Quiet street in Jerez.

September 8th, and the fiesta is held close to that date. Every year it is dedicated to a country which is a good customer for sherry. In 1956 it was dedicated to England and in 1958 to Ireland. In the seat of honour at the celebrations is the Queen of the Vintage, surrounded by her court, chosen from the most beautiful girls of Jerez and those from the country to which the vintage is dedicated, so that the mystery and dark beauty of the suntanned Andalusian girls is seen side by side with the very different beauty of the fair girls from the North.

When it gets under weigh there is every sort of fun: luncheon parties, dinner parties and parties in the park; innumerable bullfights with the finest matadors in Spain; horse shows; concerts; dances—there is no time to sleep. It all begins on the Sunday with the beautiful ceremony in which the grapes are blessed outside the churrigueresque collegiate church. After the service the queen assembles with her court at the top of the steps in front of the church. A procession of clergy and acolytes files out, bearing the image of San Gines de la Jara, the patron saint of the vintage. The priest gives his blessing; the queen casts a bucket of grapes into a wire press and the workmen slowly mark time. There is no hurry. Steadily the grapes are crushed and soon the first drops of must trickle down into the empty butt. Then suddenly the air is filled with doves, flying across Spain and carrying verses composed by local poets to tell the world that the vintage has begun. The bells ring jubilantly from the mudejar tower. A Te Deum is sung to thank the Lord for the birth of wine and the crowds slowly go away.

Panem et circenses! At night the whole town makes haste to the Feria. And then there are the fireworks—there are always fireworks in Spain. They bang and explode. It is all very haphazard. 'But what of fall-out?' There is a shrug of the shoulders. We take another glass of wine.

More about life in Jerez is to be found in Julian Jeff's book 'Sherry'.

Province of Port

by Claire Feuerheerd

Few people are better qualified to describe northern Portugal and the vintage than Claire Feuerheerd, writing from her own Quinta on the Douro below Pinhao.

During the last few years Portugal, Britain's oldest ally, has taken a high place amongst the tourist countries. In fact the *Algarve* her southernmost Province, and the districts around Lisbon of Sintra, Cascais and Estoril are rapidly becoming Little England.

The north of the country and incidentally the most beautiful part of it, has been sadly neglected, particularly the Province of *Traz-os-Montes,* to my mind the most beautiful and interesting of them all.

Traz-os-Montes ('Behind the Mountains') is bounded on two sides by the Douro valley and on the other two sides by the *Marao* range and the hills on the Spanish border. The whole district is a conglomeration of hills, schist in the valley and granite in the uplands. It is in these uplands that the Egyptian vultures have their homes. Beautiful big black and white birds with bright yellow heads; they sit by the sides of the roads or in the fields, looking like fat old gentlemen having a picnic. Here also the storks come in summer and the golden orioles with their lovely liquid whistle and bright yellow and black bodies flashing in and out among the trees. Bee-eaters and kingfishers flourish; and so unfortunately do the hawks, a menace to the smaller birds.

During the last thirty years great strides have been made in afforestation; hillsides that were bare thirty years ago are now thickly wooded. This has brought the wolves back to the *Traz-os-Montes* where in the winter they attack the flocks. The local breed of sheep dogs are trained to fight them and I heard of one who, in alliance with his shepherd, killed twenty wolves in one season. He used to make a frontal attack while the shepherd killed the wolf by clubbing it on the head with a heavy stick from behind. The dogs wear heavy spiked collars and have their ears docked.

The wild flowers of *Traz-os-Montes* are a delight. In the early part of the year (February and March) the miniature wild daffodils are in bloom. I have found nine varieties of these within a day's drive of Pinhao. In the north west corner of the Province stands Montalegre, on the borders of *Traz-os-Montes* and *Minho,* surrounded by hayfields and water meadows. In this district there are many unusual wild flowers, amongst them *Aquilegia Dichroa, Anarrhinum, Duriminium, Linaria Sapphirina, Digitalis Thapsi, Hispidella Hispanica* and *Knautia Nevadensis.* This is where the mountain cattle are bred; beautiful creatures with big gentle eyes and long sweeping horns.

The Port vintage generally starts between the middle and the end of September, the wine being made in the age-old way—carried and trodden as wine was carried and trodden in the days of Isaiah—to the sound of music, singing and shouting with nights of dancing both in and out of wine.*

After the vintage is over, the year's work in the vineyard begins. First, hoeing round the roots to let in the rains and destroy the surface roots, which take the strength from the big tap root on which the vine lives. Then the pruning, done by a specially trained gang of men who work even in the rain, protected by straw capes and leggings. At this time too, old and dead vines are replaced. Holes, one metre square, are dug to receive the young American vine on whose roots the wine-producing varieties have been grafted. This has to be done because the root of the American vine is resistant to the *Phylloxera,* the bug which found its way over here in the latter part of the last century and devastated the vineyards of Europe. Grafting last year's American stock is another job and

Cask making in Crofts' Lodges at Vila Nova de Gaia (Oporto).

211

This young picker's glowing smile disguises the back-breaking nature of the work.

then all vines have to be tied down to their wires. Now the olive oil is made; most properties grow olive trees as well as vines. Next on the list of work comes the big spring hoeing and the valley seems to wake up again with the men singing a traditional song, question and answer from gang to gang, echoing across the valleys. During the hoeing the vineyard is fertilised. We use chemicals now and a third of the vineyard is done yearly. By now the vine is shooting, and spraying begins; sulphur against oidium and Bordeaux mixture against mildew. Then one last hoeing to dig in the last of the weeds. But hoeing on the steep stone-ridden slopes is not the gentle exercise associated with an English herbaceous border. It would be better named 'hacking' and the men 'hack' from dawn to dusk.

The next two months in the vineyards are used for repairs and renewals, and for the drying and preserving of the summer fruits. Then, as the rains in the high mountains cease, the golden river turns to olive green and the level falls. Hot summer is here. We watch vines and weather hopefully; until suddenly it is September again and one evening the valley fills with music as the people come down again for the vintage.

But first everyone is scrubbing, cleaning, sweeping, whitewashing, for we are about to entertain a God. Bacchus is due next week and we expect him to stay for a fortnight. The long, tiring year is at an end; what sort of wine will our twelve months' toil bring forth?

This of course finally depends upon the year's weather, yet the vine—like most other plants—is sensitive to its environment. Here, up the Douro, a vineyard on one side of the river may be first class, whereas another, on the other side, may be second. This is partly aspect—how and when the sun strikes its terraced slope, partly soil and a great deal to do with the species of vines planted. The more the merrier has point, provided quality of the wine (colour and sugar are the first objectives) is always the primary consideration; quantity must always be second.

The peasants have their own ways of telling the first-class vineyards. Standing on the hilltops under the full moon, the vineyards either shine or look dead in the moonlight. Shun the shiny ones is what they say. One year, after a great snowstorm in February, I formed another. Standing on the road behind my quinta as the snow was melting, had I known nothing of the Douro, I could have picked all the first *quintas*. They were those where the snow had *already* melted.

But back to our visitor!

One evening just as the night is falling, music sounds along the road and down from the hills come the *roga,* a gang of rather trampish looking people, who have often walked all day from their homes in the mountains. Some are nicely drunk, some tired, but all are very cheerful. There is singing, dancing and cheering, a good supper and then bed, because tomorrow will be a hard day.

Before dawn the bell rings. The bell is an old piece of railway line hung on a wire and banged with any bit of metal handy. Everyone gets up, meeting in the long house among the granite tanks where we tread the wine. They eat some bread and have a tot of *aguadente bagaceira* (the Marc du Porto as opposed to the Marc du Bourgogne) and then we wait.

'Why is the priest so late?' He is coming to bless the vintage and he promised to be here by 7 a.m. Better ring him up. 'He's so sorry, he's so sorry, he's just coming but he was out at a 'festa' till 4 a.m. and he has overslept.' At last a cacophony of barking dogs heralds his arrival. A charming elderly man, like Dom Camillo, and adored by his flock. He blesses the presses and the vines, he gives a little sermon to the *roga,* wishes us a good crop and hurries away.

Now the women with their small baskets, go off to the vineyards followed by the train of small boys who are the plague of every *quinta*. The women cut the grapes, looking over every bunch, removing diseased or overburnt grapes (raisins go in but there is a degree of burning which chars them like wood), putting the bunches into their small baskets, which in turn fill the big baskets weighing 130 lb. carried by the men on their necks at a run as they shout an old, old call which sounds like the Bacchic shout 'Evoe'. All day long the grapes come in and by evening one of the big stone tanks *(lagar)* is full. At this stage a test is

New wine being brought down from the Douro vineyards, to the port wine lodges.

The village of Riba Longa near the junction of rivers Tua and Douro.

A worker in Croft's Lodges.

taken of the juice of the grape, the *lagrima* (tears). We use the Baumé scale for the sugar and the temperature is taken. This test is repeated after the wine ferments and has become 'must'. As the wine goes on fermenting, losing sugar and gaining alcohol, it is rested and worked by the men's feet, or else by wooden *macacos* (monkeys) like the old-fashioned wooden sticks for washing clothes. When the sugar density has decreased to the necessary degree, the wine is drawn off into the big tunnels in the building under the pressing house and there the brandy—a pure grape alcohol—is added to stop the fermentation.

But before fermentation can begin satis-factorily, the grapes must be broken up. After

supper the men, barefooted and washed from knee to toe, climb into the *lagar* and the famous treading begins. We know how much wine each 'lagar' holds in pipes (a pipe is 550 litres) and the minimum number of men per pipe needed to start the treading is $1\frac{1}{2}$, although we put in many more. The claim in Isaiah, 'I have trodden the wine press alone' is im-possible; in fact, a miracle as far as the Douro is concerned, for one man's efforts would be insufficient.

After the grapes are broken up, all join in the dancing which goes on in and out of the wine till 1 a.m. Then the roll is called and we rest till dawn. Some gangs have a mock funeral on one night during the vintage. The corpse is

217

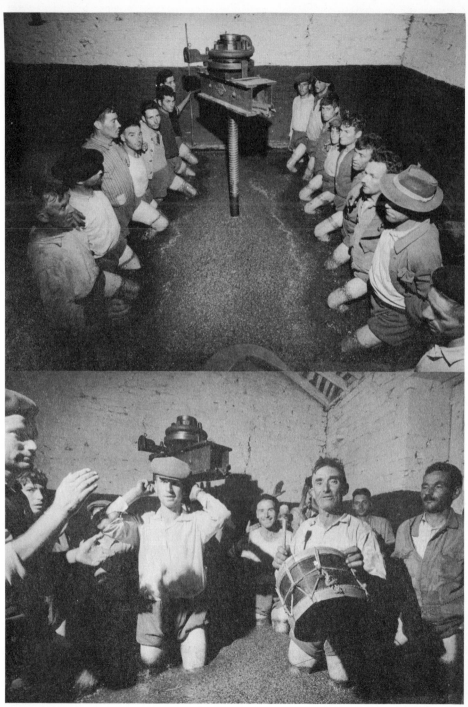

The Treading. 'Barefooted and washed from knee to toe'.

'All join in the dancing . . . in and out of the wine till 1 a.m.'.

A Peasant picker.

carried round with weeping and wailing and bell, book and candle. Suddenly the corpse comes to life, chasing everyone within sight, shrieking into the night. They have no idea, these peasant actors that they are enacting the death of the King of the Harvest. No one who has read Fraser's *The Golden Bough* can doubt it and I always have a slight shiver when I see it done. So old, so very old; and one **has** to think of Adonis and the Corn King and of Bacchus and Ariadne.

The end is the giving of the *Ramo*. The *Ramo* also takes us back to Pagan times. It is given to the owner of the quinta on the last night of vintage, decorated with grapes, paper streamers and biscuits by the *roga* who are going away. I am always given some cigarettes on mine as I am a chain smoker. This gives me a lump in my throat for my *roga* are not rich, far from it. They make a little speech to which one answers, 'Till this day next year and God be with you'. Then they dance and go away, back to their hill villages or on to other vintages in the valley, always singing, always cheering, always happy, but for us this year 'their vintage shouting has ceased'.

Mechanisation is now slowly replacing the traditional treading.

RODNEY SYMES

American Journey

by Paul Dauthieu

It is fitting to end this anthology with the one written contribution which 'The Man who *was* Peter Dominic' made to WINEMINE.

In 1964, on a trip to the United States with his wife and daughter, Rosemary, he reported his impressions in a series of letters which were circulated within the company. This article was extracted from them, omitting injunctions to the staff not to drink the profits in the Boss's absence and other domestic matter.

For the moment, this colossal ship, the 'Queen Elizabeth', is a fantastic experience. She is about as big as the Savoy Hotel, and if you can imagine that belting across the Atlantic at thirty miles an hour with little, if any, loss of its normal arts of service and entertainment such as head waiters making bonfires of pancakes and cabaret dancers hurling each other through the air with the greatest of ease, then you have more imagination than I had. Of course, the sea no doubt is still the master but we have been lucky so far.

BIGGER GLASSES

At lunchtime there is free wine—Algerian, but not bad at all. Château Margaux 1955 is to be had at 31s 6d a bottle. As ever there is something to crusade for in wine; in this case larger glasses—they will use silly little sherry-size glasses for table wine although they have the right type—8 or 9-ounce Paris goblets—reserved exclusively for Champagne. WE now have these for our claret and three other tables so far have now boldly demanded them too. If you want people to drink wine, why not give them the biggest glasses you can get away with?

Looking back to Southampton, there must be scope too for a gift service of Bon Voyage bottles. Literally tons of flowers were carried on board this ship, but little or no champagne.

Now we approach New York, capital of a nation of 'hard liquor' drinkers who yet manage to drink *five* bottles of wine per head per year against our 2¼: There must surely be some 'know-how' which we in Britain lack. Perhaps we shall discover the secret.

CARS WITH COMPASSES

It is now two weeks since we landed and after being fried brown at 80 to 86°F. for a week in New York, we were glad to leave, even though escape involved a battle of wits with murderous traffic, cunningly deceptive road signs and unfamiliarity with a hired car. It took almost two hours to reach a reasonably clear roadway (not more than three abreast!)

Motoring on the American super 'thru-ways' one becomes a piece of flotsam floating furiously on the automobile tide. We hoped to drift towards Boston, but the direction signs merely said 'West' or 'North' omitting place names. I can only suppose American cars are fitted with compasses.

Eventually we were decanted through a graceful figure of eight designed to defeat any compass, into a delightful 'small time' seaport called New London on Thames. A room one floor up in the very comfortable Lighthouse Inn was far better than the 39th floor in New York with Broadway far below.

KNEW DOMINIC

The 'Great White Way', I regret, turns out to be rather tawdry, and extremely smelly. It looks best from far above—say the 86th floor of the Empire State building! Of course, these immensely tall buildings are certainly impressive—the skyline entering New York harbour is an unforgettable first experience; especially as the quays are almost in the centre of the city and we could actually see the ship's funnels from our bedroom windows. The Hilton in London looks tall, with thirty floors, and its roof-top restaurant gives a remarkable view of London. But in New York we were constantly eating in restaurants far higher than that; in one case at the 65th floor, and with a 'window-table' incidentally, because the manager knew the name 'Dominic'! He had emigrated from London seven years ago after being head-waiter at the Mirabelle in the 'forties.

By and large, the food is good, if somewhat stereotyped, but much more lyrically listed than artistically cooked. The 'sales pressure' is always full on, and no one dreams of calling a spade merely a spade. A lettuce on any menu is, at the very least, 'A generous wedge of crispiest tender green New England lettuce, with Thousand Island dressing'; and whatever that may be, what turns up, of course, is simply a lettuce —though usually a good one.

ELUSIVE WINE LIST

But the most unnerving experience is confrontation with a large glass of iced water the moment one sits down at table—whether breakfast, lunch, tea, or dinner. And it is quite useless to refuse it. Almost equally difficult is to see the Wine List. No effort is made to encourage wine drinking, which is curious, for fantastic sums are spent dolling up the so-called sommeliers in fancy uniforms. At New York's Waldorf-Astoria there was a cunning old French fox dressed like a Gilbertian Admiral and weighed down with a key and chain large enough to have been removed from the 'Queen Elizabeth's' cable deck. But he will not expect to sell anything more than 'King-size Martinis' and Champagne ('American or French, we have 'em all!') The Wine List, extracted almost at gunpoint, turned out to be a magnificent parchment sheet rolled up on a 2-foot Admiral's baton.

WHIT-MONDAY WATER

The Liquor shops in the towns we have seen are just what the name implies and no more. They show almost nothing but spirits and obviously do not expect to sell wine; yet the mystery remains—America drinks more wine a head a year than we do.

Under Canada's State Controlled Liquor laws, her towns have nothing to show in the way of wine merchants. The 'Liquor Stores' are few and bare; pass through the turnstile, get your ticket, consult price sheet, write down what you want on the ticket, wait for it, pay at the door and push off. If you don't like the brand, or the price, you can lump it and probably get your licence endorsed for insolence. And of course no 'likker' on Sundays at all. Even in Toronto on Whit-Monday— Victoria Day to them—we could get only water.

From Toronto to Niagara Falls—a magnificent sight, even if it did mean even more blasted water, but at Buffalo we were back in the United States and could at least get our 'likker' on demand.

SOMETHING TO LEARN

We have now spent four fascinating days in Chicago, to me a far more attractive city than New York. There are wide, clean, business-like streets, and a fine main shopping avenue looking over gardens to Lake Michigan. We looked over the Lake from one of the Conrad Hilton's 3,000 rooms, admiring the efficiency with which 2,000 guests were vacated when some Convention ended suddenly. A battery of fourteen lifts under female 'dispatchers' coped with this exodus. I felt the departing guests should all have had flight numbers.

Here in Chicago we have at last found something to learn. The town has had no Retail Price Maintenance for many years. It has been—and is—'catch as catch can'; no doubt this may have arisen from Capone methods, though I have never seen any town less suggestive of gangsters. The result has been the emergence of a few very large, well organised competitive liquor stores, run on super-market lines. Two of these each have 100 by 80 feet of floor space and 20 assistants dancing attendance upon it. So, at long last, perhaps we have a clue to the mystery of U.S. wine consumption.

Paul Dauthieu, the founder of Peter Dominic.